THE TOP TEN
Preschool Parenting
PROBLEMS

and what to do about them!

Roslyn Ann Duffy

TOP 10
Preschool Parenting
PROBLEMS
and what to do about them!

These articles originally appeared in *Exchange — The Early Childhood Leaders'
Magazine*. *Exchange* is a bimonthly management magazine for directors and owners of
early childhood programs. For more information about *Exchange* and other Exchange
publications for directors and teachers, contact:

Exchange
PO Box 3249
Redmond, WA 98073-3249
(800) 221-2864
www.ChildCareExchange.com

ISBN 978-0-942702-48-4

Printed in the United States of America

Cover Photograph by Timothy Firth

DEDICATION

I dedicate this book, with love, to my family —
and, with blessings, to yours.

ALSO BY ROSLYN DUFFY

Positive Discipline for Preschoolers
(with Jane Nelsen and Cheryl Erwin)
New York: Three Rivers Press, 2007

Positive Discipline the First Three Years
(with Jane Nelsen and Cheryl Erwin)
New York: Three Rivers Press, 2007

Positive Discipline: A Teacher's A-Z Guide
(with Jane Nelsen and others)
Roseville, CA: Prima Publishers, 2001

The Parent Report Card
(with Elizabeth Crary)
Parenting Press, 2001

Positive Discipline for Preschooler's Facilitator's Guide
(with Jane Nelsen, and Mary Hughes)
Empowering People Books, Tapes, and Videos, 2000

ACKNOWLEDGEMENTS

My friend, Lily, once told me about a Chinese concept known as, 'Back Mountain,' made up of the people who stand behind us — offering support, encouragement, and love. I know for a fact that my 'Back Mountain' is a whole mountain range! The following are only a few of my incredible 'Back Mountain' landscape.

Thank you, Lynn, for long ago seeing something in me that I still struggle to see in myself; to Bonnie for the opportunity to write my 'From a Parent's Perspective' column, which forms the foundation of this book; and to Jane and Cheryl for expanding my world through our many writing years together on the *Positive Discipline* titles.

A big thank you to Laurie for beginning the Learning Tree Montessori School with me and to the staff and families who have shared their lives with us, so enriching ours, these many years.

Thank you Lily, for your 'only in America' observation, that began our shared magic carpet adventures and opened so many doors — as well as my eyes.

Thank you to Carole and Scott for making this book into the beautiful creation it is and to those who read this manuscript in its very earliest incarnation: Laura Holt, Kitty Brown, Laura Knapp — for their thoughts which helped shape the final version of the book and their encouragement which made it first seem real. And thank you my dearest KK, for your faithful weekly phone calls — they truly kept me going.

Finally, my love and thanks to my mom and dad, and to my truest teachers — our children: Blue, Manus, Rose, and Bridget; their spouses, Pete and Celeste; and of course to my 'grand'children: Mia, Maria, and Genevieve, who have given me the chance to see the world all over again — through their eyes.

And most of all, to my very first reader, idea person, and the one who keeps reminding me to 'write the book!' — all my love to you — Vinnie.

TABLE OF CONTENTS

The Top Ten
Preschool Parenting Problems

#1 to #4:
Like banging an elbow, some things can really make you want to scream.
These first and highest-ranking problems do this well.

1   **WHINING** *tops almost every list as the #1 problem behavior. How can that high-pitched little voice wield so much power? Even more relevant — why does whining work so well? Here are some thoughts:*

2   **NOT LISTENING** or **NON-COMPLIANCE**: *What we really mean when we say a child doesn't listen is that she doesn't do what she is told to do; hence NOT LISTENING and NON-COMPLIANCE merge into problem #2. Let's take a closer look at some typical situations:*

3   **MELTDOWNS — FRUSTRATIONS** and **TANTRUMS**: *When the whining doesn't work for your child and listening isn't working for either or both of you, problem #3 is easy to predict because someone is going to MELTDOWN.*

4   **NEGOTIATION** and **MANIPULATION**: *Exactly when does negotiation stop and manipulation begin? Let's see how desperate or clever they, and we, can get.*

#5 to #8:

Now we come to the most crowded section of this book. Problems #5 through #8 may not have the tortuous intensity of the first 4, but they sure can wear us down. These next problems are those daily things we slog through, from getting up in the morning, through brushing teeth and bolting down bagels, to diaper duty and bath or bedtime battles — 24/7.

5a   **MORNING HASSLES**

Go. Go. Go. Hurry. Hurry. Hurry. No! No! No! And, thus, the day begins.

5b MEALTIME MISCHIEF

Meals with little ones can give a whole new meaning to 'messy.'

5c BEDTIME BLUES: *Day is done, but does sleep seem like a foggy memory? Whether dealing with bedtime battles or midnight wakings, if you peer out at each new day through weary eyes — here is a bedtime prescription.*

6 SIBLING FIGHTS: *The good news is that if you only have one child, you can skip this chapter since the only people who list this problem have more than one child. But with more than one child — there are going to be, well, issues! Think 'relationships and skills' instead of 'whodunit' and you'll be on the right track.*

7 CLEAN-UP and CHORES: *Problem #7 is shared: by the double whammies of CLEAN-UP and CHORES. Let's start at the very beginning, as we welcome baby . . .*

8   **BATHROOM BATTLES** *team up for a double-header as problem #8 — with most innings getting played out in the bathroom.*

#9 and #10:

At this point, we move from defiance to flat-out provocation (or at least what most adults interpret as such). Whether children mean to be hurtful, are feeling frustrated or hurt themselves, or simply want attention — these behaviors get us in the gut.

9   **HURTING BEHAVIORS**: *Sometimes behaviors get out-of-control (ours and theirs), with someone or something getting hurt.*

10   **BAD** LANGUAGE: *Problem #10 combines everything from Potty Talk to Swearing to Name-Calling. It doesn't take long for children to discover the impact of a well-placed bad word — but there is also an aspect of humor to this early word use; if you want to hear children chuckle, just mention farts, poop, or booties.*

More Problems:

We have made it through 10 of The Top Ten Preschool Parenting Problems, but there are **MORE PROBLEMS** *that emerge in these early years. In this section we look at:*

ADULT ISSUES: *Many problems are unique to adults.*

FAMILY ISSUES: *Children transform us into families, but how do we connect with this new creation?*

HARD TOPICS: *Challenges come in many forms: some of them we can anticipate (like providing information about awkward topics such as sex), but many we cannot (divorce, separation, death, or illness) — and they change everything.*

Universal Tools:

Whatever the problem affecting child or adult, certain basic tools will help.
Here are some you don't want to do without:

INTRODUCTION

In the Beginning

For most of my life I have been around young children and families. My experiences have ranged from raising my own four children; to beginning and running the Learning Tree, one of the first all-day Montessori child care programs in the United States; to leading parenting classes and working with families through my counseling practice. For years I have listened to and grappled with the problems we share. Whether in my own life, with teachers, or with parents, we have worked together to find effective and healthy ways to encourage children and ourselves through these awesome growing-up years and beyond.

In online parenting chats on AOL and Moms Online, or in my call-in question and answer talks for NPR (and other) radio programs, I have heard the concerns, struggles, and worries of parents with children of all ages. And my work through the World Forum on Early Care and Education, with families and educators from over 80 countries, has given me the unique chance to hear concerns from other cultures, as well. The truth is that we are often more alike than we are different.

A topic such as getting children ready in the morning may involve convincing a child not to wear shorts and sandals on a snowy day in Michigan; rushing to get a child to the curb in time for his child care shuttle bus in downtown Athens; or coaxing a child to eat her rice before heading out the door on a warm Singapore morning. No matter where in the world it is happening — our problems have amazing universal resonance.

Thinking about all of these experiences, I realized that what this work is really about are the problems we share. The Top Ten Preschool Parenting Problems represents my bringing together these many points of view. This book is about each of us, your struggles and mine, and the real life solutions we find or seek to find, for our everyday dilemmas. It is our common imperfections and humanity — and the problems we share, that are the true heart of this book.

How To Use This Book
By now you have probably scanned to find YOUR particular #1 Parenting Problem. If, however, you have identified three or more problems — my suggestion is to head to the **More Problems** section and read 'No Hang Time'; 'A Time to Laugh'; 'Kindling'; or 'What About Sex?' before you read about those other problems. Just maybe, tending to hearts and spirits (yours and others) will help to whittle down that initial list of problems.

Only What Matters
This book comes with an additional and unique permission — you don't have to read it all! Parents of young children are busy, probably sleepy, and often overwhelmed. This is not the kind of book that you need to read from cover to cover or add to that list of things you're feeling guilty about not doing. Find the issue(s) you need help with, turn to that page or pages and get some fresh ideas (or maybe be reminded of ones you already know). Interwoven in every topic are solid principles for parenting, teaching, and living together — that can make our lives and our enjoyment of one another much, much nicer.

For those of you who want more of the underpinnings, the philosophical and intellectual basis for many of the tools you will read about here, please consider the information you can find in my other books: *Positive Discipline: The First Three Years*; or *Positive Discipline for Preschoolers* (both co-authored with Jane Nelsen and Cheryl Erwin, Three Rivers Press, Random House) and *Positive Disciple: A Teacher's A to Z Guide* (co-authored with numerous others, also Three Rivers Press, Random House).

My Caveat

To protect the privacy of my own family and others whose stories I use, I have changed names, places, and details. Some examples may be a blend of several situations or only based on snippets of an assortment of stories. Each example is meant to illustrate information and make it easier to understand, rather than being verbatim accounts or precise re-tellings.

Now sit back and please READ ON.

#1

Whining

Whining tops almost every list as the
#1 problem behavior.
How can that high-pitched little voice
wield so much power?
Even more relevant — why does whining work so well?
Here are some thoughts.

Pass on the "Whine"

Situation: Too Much 'Whining!

For the past few years the parents in my parenting classes have chosen **whining** *as their #1 problem. Whining resembles personalized water torture, but that steady drip-drip-drip that can drive one mad is mild compared to the effect of little Agatha's daily dose of whine on her listeners.*

I try to write about issues that are bothering folks the most, but **whining** *had me stuck. I would say to myself, "But I don't know what to say about whi-i-i-nng!" Then I listened to what I was saying. Whoa! That's right. I was whining! My first revelation was —* **whining** *is not restricted to children. Excellent! I was on to something — but what?*

Solution

What is whining and why do people do it? The basic formula is — whine enough and others will: leave you alone; quit bothering you or asking you to do something you don't want to do; give you what you want; or change their behavior in some way to get you to stop whining. No wonder whining is universal. It works!

COMMUNICATION: MISTAKEN GOALS

At its most basic, **whining** is communication. The problem is that whining can communicate many different things. The cure for whining lies in both its elusiveness and variability: what is being communicated?

- I want to be noticed. (Attention)
- I want my way. (Power)
- I feel hurt. (Revenge)
- I don't matter. (Inadequacy and insignificance)

The above are all variations of what are referred to as **mistaken goals** in the *Positive Discipline* materials (for a more detailed explanation see *Positive Discipline for Preschoolers*, 2007, Random House). Mistaken goal behaviors relate to our universal need to **belong** and the ways in which people of all ages seek to get this need met — in inappropriate ways. When we respond to needs with healthy and appropriate attention, empowerment, listening and appreciation, **belonging** issues will get met, too.

EMOTIONAL NEEDS

Communication often involves feelings — but young children do not understand or express their feelings well. Some possibilities include:

- I am lonely.
- I am bored.
- I am sad (scared, nervous, frightened . . .)

Feeling messages often lurk like icebergs beneath a child's roiling demands and relentless storms of uncooperative behavior.

"I WANT . . . "

Even more basic are messages about the tangible **wants** and desires we all have.

- I want a doll.
- I want an ice cream cone.
- I want new shoes.

The trick here is figuring out the difference between a **want** and a **need** (maybe new shoes are **needed** but cowboy boots are **wanted**) and determining how to meet needs and which wants can be granted. The other detail is to avoid granting anything in response to the 'whine'.

"I NEED . . . "

Basic physical needs can be communicated through whining. A child's whining may be saying:

- I am tired.
- I am hungry.
- I don't feel well.

As the possibilities increase, it becomes obvious that whining is an excellent all-purpose communication tool — a sort of auditory cure-all. The problem is that whining does not cure problems — but creates them. Whining is about as desirable to listen to as the yapping of an insomniac Chihuahua at 2 a.m.

Whining is not music to anyone's ears –
but it continues to top the misbehavior charts!

WHINING WORKS

When something works, it gets repeated. The yapping dog, whose owner trots out day and night, to let him in or out, uses his simple canine brain cells to figure out that **yapping works**. In the same way, whining people, young or old, use their brain cells to decide that **whining works**.

If a child whines in the grocery store, begging for a candy bar and soon finds his mouth filled with melty chocolate — the **whining worked**. Will he try it again? Wouldn't you? If a child gets mom or dad or grandma to read an extra story at bedtime for little more effort than a high-pitched "Just one m-ooo-rrrree, pl-eeeaaa-ssssse. Mommm——-mm-eeeeeeee!'" (As you read this, imagine crystal shattering on that final '-eeeeeeee!')

Whining does, indeed, work. Haven't I managed to avoid writing about whining for years — even though I am the only one I had been whining to about not knowing what to say? Now that is pretty effective whining, if I do say so myself!

TOO MUCH WHINE

As with most frustrations, a good initial response is to take a deep breath. As that first shrill tendril of sound snakes its way into your consciousness, breathe in slowly (two or three times, if need be). Then suggest to your child that she take a deep breath, too. Show her how to do so.

Now ask her to tell you what she needs in a clear voice. Don't mention the whine — focus on what you want to hear.

APPROPRIATE ATTENTION

Make that deep breath (yours and hers) the starting point. Then make clear communication the goal. What is needed? Is this about **wants**?

"I want a cookie. Please."

"That was a very nice way to ask. Thank you. You [may have a cookie now; after bath time; when we finish dinner (or whatever response is appropriate)]."

By responding to the well-spoken request instead of reacting to the initial whining, the behavior you want will get appropriate attention and the whining will not. Whining stops working.

'NEEDS' NEED ACTION

If the need is physical or a child is in distress — action, not words are needed. The child whining in the grocery aisle may well be tired and in need of a nap. Take action. Get him to a quiet place where he can rest and recharge. There is little point in doing your own whining about a child's whining or punishing him and making increased demands on his behavior if his ability to comply is compromised. Tired children need rest.

A whining, hungry child needs food. Pull out the crackers, nuts, or raisins that you keep on hand and deal with the hunger — pass on the whine.

If the need is physical, meet it with action — not words —

as in threats, bribes, and lectures.

FEELINGS

Emotional needs are even less easy to articulate. Feelings require understanding and validation. A lonely, bored, or nervous child does not need a lecture.

If mom and dad are going out and Margo the high school sophomore from down the hall is babysitting —— little Betty's whining may be her way of saying that she is sad, lonely, or nervous. Come to a full stop. Give Betty the understanding she needs by responding to her real **emotional** message and not its annoying delivery.

"I don't want this ni-i-i-ghtgo-o-own."
"These eggs are icc—ccckkkk-yyyy. I wanted p-aaa-aann-caaa-kkes!"
"I don't wa-a-aaannnt Mar-rr-ggg-ooo to baby-sit. Don't G-OOO-OO!"

Stop. Breathe. Interpret.

"You seem very upset. Maybe what we really need is some hug time. Help me [put this nightgown away; clear the table], and then let's sit and hug for a bit."
By going straight to a child's distress message, instead of its delivery style, and asking the child to help in some way (thus creating a feeling of belonging — that crucial basic need — through contribution) — further whining will disappear. While cuddling, talk about it being okay to ask for a hug sometimes. This adds a skill to replace the whining.

Did the whining work? Did it change the clothing or menu? No. Did the message get interpreted? Yes.

Understanding makes whining unnecessary.

SOOTHING SOUNDS

Whining can be many things. Take a few deep breaths. Respond to appropriate behavior — not the **whine**. Take action in response to physical needs. Offer understanding and teach skills to address emotional needs.

What doesn't work — won't get repeated.

#2

Not Listening/Non-Compliance

What we really mean when we say a child
doesn't listen *is that she doesn't do*
what she is told to do; hence,
NOT LISTENING and NON-COMPLIANCE
merge into TOP 10 problem #2.
Let's take a closer look at some typical situations.

How Many Times
Do I Have To Tell You . . . ?

Situation: How Many Times . . .

"Jimmy, where is your lunchbox? How many times do I have to remind you . . . ?"

"Betsy, put your baby sister down! Haven't I told you . . . ?"

"Margo, marking pens aren't allowed in the living room. If I've told you once, I've told you a hundred times . . . !"

Solution: Who is the Slow Learner?

"How many times. . . . " "Haven't I told you. . . . " "I've told you a hundred times. . . . " Don't you have to wonder who the slow learner might be here? When we do the same thing over and over, with the same results time after time — maybe it's time to rethink what we are doing.

If you have to remind little Jimmy, day after day, to bring home his lunchbox — whose job has remembering the lunchbox become?

When Betsy walks across the kitchen holding her baby sister, what are the chances that she doesn't know that this is forbidden?

If you have told Margo "a hundred times" not to bring marking pens into the living room — has she missed hearing you every time? Of course we all forget and do things we should remember not to do or forget to do things we should do — but the bigger question is, "Why do we adults keep doing the same thing, time after frustrating time?".

IF IT DOESN'T WORK . . .

When something hasn't worked — why repeat it? If the toaster shorted out — would you put bread in it every morning? A broken toaster is easy to understand. We can laugh at the folly of putting bread in it and expecting toast. And yet, isn't that what we do when we repeat ineffective behaviors over and over again, even though the results don't change — then we blame the child's response instead of our approach? Let's step back and take a fresh look.

REMINDERS

Reminders tend to transfer responsibility to the person doing the reminding. If Jimmy doesn't mind taking his lunch to school in a plastic or paper bag — why should you? When or if using his lunchbox matters to him — he will remember it. If you can't let go of this issue — talk it over. Ask him what would help him to remember. Maybe he could make a list that he carries in his pocket and checks before getting on the school bus at the end of each day. The word lunchbox or a picture of one could remind him to retrieve his before leaving. Or he could place his coat on top of his lunchbox to help him remember (although this raises the risk of returning home with neither coat nor lunchbox).

Make your goal that of helping Jimmy to come up with a plan for remembering his things. Limit your involvement to supporting that plan. **Remembering** becomes his job, while **reminding** will no longer be part of yours.

ASK

Have you told Betsy not to pick up her baby sister? Of course you have. If your child knows a rule — don't repeat it, ask instead: "Betsy, what is the rule about picking your sister up?" "Why do we have that rule?" "What will help you to remember that rule?" These questions convey two important messages. The first is that we have confidence in this child's intelligence and ability to remember the rule. The second is that we are expressing confidence in her ability to follow that rule in the future. Both invite a child to feel confident and capable. Rather nice bonuses while securing little sister's safety.

ACT

If a rule gets violated over and over again, and the child does know what the rule is, then action instead of words are called for. In the example of the marking pens, if Margo knows she is not to bring the pens into the living room and does so anyway, then have her help you gather the pens or gather them yourself and remove them. When she begins to complain (a high probability), ask her what the rule about marking pens is. When she responds that they aren't allowed in the living room and most likely adds that "I forg-o-o—t-t", commiserate with her and assure her that you have confidence she will remember tomorrow when the pens will, once again, be available.

It is important to spell out what you will do if a rule is broken (before it gets broken). Please pay attention to that last sentence. It says **what you will do**. This is an important distinction.

If you say that you will put the pens away for the rest of that day, then you can do so. Doing so is within your control. If you say that she will have to pick the pens up and give them to you — you cannot really make this happen; instead, you have opened the door to a power struggle. By aiming attention at getting a child to do something (pick up the pens), we also set ourselves up to **reward** her refusal to do so with more (albeit negative) attention.

By focusing on **what you will do**, you can avoid a power struggle and reduce inappropriate attention. When this is done without threats and while offering reassurance that you trust she will do better next time, you model respectful behavior and invite her self-confidence.

COMMUNICATE

An adult's exasperated "how many times" is soon tuned-out: *there she goes again.* When we repeat things over and over, we actually invite others to quit listening. They've heard it before — why do so again?

That may mean asking a child to come to you or you going to where she is, looking her in the eye, or getting down to her level by sitting or kneeling next to her. Whispering (though seemingly counter-intuitive) also works to get a child to tune-in to what is being said. Once you have her attention — then talk.

Such one-on-one communication prevents a child's humiliation and conveys respect — something we can't model often enough.

> *When we have something to say that matters, we need to say it in a way that matters.*

GET CREATIVE

Let's go back to the idea that something we say or do isn't working. What else can we do? Sometimes we feel stuck, that we have "tried everything" and "nothing works".

First of all, EVERYTHING is a BIG word. Even though you may not have thought of them, there are other ways to do things. Challenge yourself to come up with at least three ideas, even if they seem silly or impractical.

What are three ideas Margo's mom might do to address the marking pen problem? How about:

- Replace all marking pens with colored pencils that can be used in the living room.
- Set up a drawing table in a corner of the living room, restricting the use of markers to that space.
- Install special marker alarms in the living room so a siren goes off every time a marker passes through the doorway.

(Of course there isn't such a thing as a marker alarm, but if you invent one I think there might be a market). The point is that it is okay to be a little silly because coming up with *any* ideas at all will help to get thinking **unstuck**.

CHANGING THE ENVIRONMENT

Analyze situations that occur over and over again and look for ways to prevent them from turning into problems. We've already come up with solutions to the marking pens problem. In the lunchbox example, switching to paper lunch bags might work.

Allowing Betsy to hold her sister while sitting down with an adult next to her would improve her skills and address the underlying issue of safety while providing positive interactions between the sisters and boosting Betsy's self-confidence. These are great win-win outcomes.

BECOME A LEARNER

If you have done/said/tried something "a hundred times" and didn't like the results — try something else. Learn from what doesn't work and find something that does. If you can't fix that broken toaster — replace it.

If what you do doesn't work — change it/change the situation/or change your expectations.

When it hasn't worked the past 99 times — maybe it's time to ask why.

Time To Go —
Say It, Do It

Situation: Time To Go — If You Say It, Do It

"Angela, if you throw that ball one more time — we're leaving!"

"Benjamin James, what did I say? If you can't share the sandbox toys, we're going home!"

"Micah, I warned you we'd have to leave if you took that toy away from your sister. If this is the way you behave, we aren't coming back to Auntie Cathy's again!"

Solution: So Leave!

Do those statements sound a bit too familiar? Children everywhere hear such messages all the time: then little Angela will toss her ball — again; little Benjamin will continue to stockpile the sandbox shovels; and wily Micah will snatch first a rattle, then a spinning top, and next a cuddly bunny out of his baby sister, Lucy's, tiny fingers. Their parents' messages and the children's behavior will continue — but nothing changes: no one stops and no one goes.

SAY IT — DO IT

Doing what we say is called **follow-through** and most of us aren't very good at it. The reason why what we **say** and **do** often fail to match is because most of us suffer from the **Too Much Syndrome**. This syndrome comes in three recognizable forms. We ask **Too Much**; say **Too Much**; or say we will do **Too Much** (more than we are willing to really do).

ASK TOO MUCH

When we tell a young child that there will be dire consequences if he or she does something "one more time", we have spelled out almost certain disaster. Why? Impulse control.

Young children don't have much impulse control or are working on acquiring it. Throwing that ball "one more time" is almost a reflex action. A better plan would be to say what to do with the ball: "Keep the ball on the floor. Please roll it along the ground."

If that fails to work — ask the child how she needs to play with the ball when inside. This method gets the child engaged in the problem and makes it easier for her to comply.

If the problem continues, act. Take the ball away. Assure her she will have a chance to try to use it in an acceptable way later that day (or the next day, or whatever seems reasonable).

If after you have done these things and problems continue, it is time to leave. You said it. Now do it. *So go.*

SAYING TOO MUCH

Does Benjamin's mom really believe he doesn't know what she said? His mom has become very practiced at repeating things, and Benjamin knows that she will keep saying it (whatever it was this time) until her voice reaches shriek level, at which point he might respond.

Mom's flow of words has long ago become background noise to Benjamin, because mom says a lot more than she does. Follow-through is rare. The words flow — but actions don't.

SAY LESS — AND MEAN MORE

Try asking a child what he thinks it is that you are going to say, in this case, about sharing the sandbox toys. Most likely, he will thrust a shovel in his playmate's direction while muttering, "I can't have them all." Or, "I have to share." (Big sigh). Let the child have a chance to say something — which will make his **doing** that something far more probable.

They do KNOW! Try asking. Here is a good self-check. Try to say what it is you want from a child in ten words (or less). Example: "It is time to leave. It is really cold today, so you need to get your coat on and then we will go outside" (24 words).

Replace the above with: "Coat," (1 word). Maybe add, "Cold," (2 words). He will know what you mean. Now go!

SAYING MORE THAN YOU WILL DO

And then we have the "You are grounded for life"; "We're never coming back to Auntie's again!"; "Get down from that tree or I'm coming up to get you"; and the "This is the last movie I am ever taking you to", category of comments. These all-inclusive statements are so over the top, even we hear how silly they sound as they slide out of our mouths like overgrown chewing gum bubbles before popping and splattering all over our faces.

That "we're never coming back" threat is one that Micah and his Auntie have probably heard more times than either of them can count. Of course Micah will be coming back to his Auntie's. Isn't this where the family will gather for Passover (or Hari Raya, or Christmas)?

When we say things like the above, we become less credible. And what about Auntie? Isn't this threatened banishment of her favorite nephew punishing her as well? The moral here is:

If you say it — be prepared to do it.

Therefore, be careful of what you say.

LEAVING — OR NOT?

If it is time to leave, be prepared to do so. Make leaving real — not a dangling threat. And remember, leaving as punishment may be punishing others besides the child. Try to deal with misbehavior in other ways, such as going into another room to help a child calm down or reviewing expected behaviors once more. If the misbehavior continues, then leave while reassuring everyone that you are confident there will be another, more successful opportunity to behave better on the next visit.

Save announcements about leaving for the few minutes before stepping out the door.

"Time to go" needs to be linked to (news flash!) — going.

One of my daughters once told me that when I said it was "time to go", she knew she had at least a half-hour to play, because I would take forever saying good-bye. You know what? She was right. I had to work at getting my own goodbyes said before I made that final leaving announcement. Then, when I said it — we left.

FOLLOW-THROUGH WORKS

If we want our children to hop up and leave when we say it is time to do so, then we need to be prepared — to go. If we want others to listen to what we say then:

*When we **say it**,*

*We need to **do it**.*

This is follow-through — and follow-through works, SO —

Beware of what you say . . .

The Car Seat Crisis

Situation: Time to Shift Gears

I am furious with my son. Our daily ride home drives us both to tears. He howls the entire way. Every evening I arrive at his child care, greet him, and we head to the car. Then the grief begins. I have to buckle him into his car seat. He arches his back, squirms, and kicks at me. I issue threats, lose my temper, and end up forcing him into the seat. He thrashes about, screams, and tries to get unbuckled.

*The same scene occurs every time we get into the car, not just after a day at child care. His safety is at issue, but I dread these constant battles. A ride of any duration while listening to him carry on prompts me to clench the steering wheel until my hands ache. I know he hates being unable to move around but he **has** to be buckled up, I can't give him any other choices. Help!*

Solution

My guess is that America's pioneers had to contend with young Caleb squawking about needing to use a saddle when he rode his horse, and sometimes Sunbonnet Susie pitched a fit when assigned to travel in the back of the wagon. Car seats create a situation unique to modern times, but the battle of wills is timeless.

Think of **C**hange, **A**ctivity, and **R**esistance. These three words sum up the situation, conjure up different solutions, and their initials conveniently spell **CAR**.

CHANGE

Change requires a gearshift. Car travel means shifting from one activity, environment, or experience to a different one. Whether moving from playtime to mealtime, storytime to bedtime, or from one place to another — all involve a change in the flow of activity. Children need extra help with such transitions. The capacity to see what is ahead helps us choose the best gear setting.

PICTURE IT

Imagine a small canvas on which you and your child create an image, but do so without paints, brushes, or paper — using words alone. This drawing provides a mental picture of the upcoming situation, with compliance part of the picture.

Talk through the activity. Ask questions. Each question and its answer applies an additional brush stroke to a child's ability to **see** the event. Let's take a look.

Before leaving the child care, paint a picture of what is ahead. Ask your child what happens when you arrive to pick him up each evening. He will likely say, "We give each other hugs." "We look at my art projects." And maybe he will say, "I don't want to go yet."

Acknowledge that he enjoys playing at school and would like to stay longer, then continue asking him what else happens. Prompt him if necessary.

"When we go outside what do we do?"
"We get in our car."
"That's right. And then what do we do?"

Eventually he will say that he needs to get into his car seat and get buckled up. Like a paint-by-number project, a clear picture of the leaving process will take form. This takes only a couple of minutes and yet it can eliminate 75 to 80 percent of the usual battles. Compare spending five minutes preparing for a transition in this way versus a half-hour or more listening to your child howl.

Some of the most positive discipline is prevention!

REAL PICTURES

A small percentage of children require more than words. Drawing a simple sketch of the upcoming activity can be helpful. Describe the activity as you draw, using stick figures and pen or pencil.

"This is Jimmy going to his car."
"This is Jimmy sitting in his car seat, all buckled up."
"This is Mommy and Jimmy riding home."

A basic three-frame drawing done in this fashion can work wonders for children who need extra visual clues.

One child care takes pictures of children involved in tasks such as putting away blocks, clearing mealtime dishes, or lying on mats at naptime. These pictures allow children to **see** expectations, making them easier to achieve.

ALERT!

Alert! Car seat! Long confinement ahead!

Is your child physically ready to sit still? Sitting in a car seat is just that — sitting. Five or ten minutes spent running, climbing, or jumping on the playground may make the next half-hour in a car seat more tolerable.

Consider playing a game in which we 'leave all our wiggles' inside before heading for the car. Join him in a fun hokey pokey shake at the door.

STARVATION AND OTHER HAZARDS OF TRAVEL

There are other physical needs to consider. Avoid the danger of anyone perishing (or threatening to) from dehydration on the ride home. Share a cup of milk, water, or juice before leaving (and be sure to trot to the bathroom for a last minute potty stop). Keep a carton of juice or water in the car for en route thirst emergencies.

Foresee starvation. Uneaten items from a lunch box make great car snacks. One car-pooling mom would arrive with a small sack of treats, and after hoisting her three little ones onto the hood of her car, would join with them, munching through the sack's contents before attempting to get anyone settled into the car.

A small bag of fruit leather, raisins, or crackers kept handy can prevent hunger meltdowns during the commute. And always include toileting as part of departure preparations. (I spent one memorable field trip at a blueberry farm with only one outhouse and 20 children. Enough said!)

RESISTANCE

The final letter of **CAR** stands for **resistance** (i.e., the power struggle). YOU want your child to sit still and buckle up while HE is busy proving that you can't make him do so. Well, the truth is — you can't, at least not permanently. Even if you do overpower him, someday he will learn how to unbuckle himself.

What you **can** control is **your** behavior. Decide what you will do and explain your decision to him ahead of time. For example, you have decided you will drive only if he is buckled into his seat. If he refuses to get buckled in (or unbuckles himself later), you will read a book and wait (remember to pull over and stop if driving, and then read and wait), until he cooperates. (Tip: Make sure it is an interesting book — even though you may forget to hold it right side up as you struggle to remain calm and silent). Silent? That's right. Say nothing. (Trust me — this is the very hardest part!)

Count on getting the opportunity to put this plan into action. The first time or two he will need to check if you really mean what you say. When he begins to struggle, open your book and read. It will take only a moment or two for him to notice that you are not responding in your usual fashion. (Even if this takes 10 or 15 minutes, it beats listening to his howls 10 or more times a week, trip after trip.) At some point he will be ready to buckle up. (A copy of *The Top Ten Preschool Parenting Problems* would make a good choice to inject a bit of encouragement into your reading and waiting time!)

Everyone wins. Fighting alone is boring. It may take a child a while to come to that conclusion, but he will. When he says he is ready: help him buckle up, turn the key, and head for the road. You will both have shifted gears. Happy travels!

RULES FOR THE ROAD

C.A.R.

Change: It is hard to change or shift one's mental and emotional gears. Use clear signals in preparation to merge smoothly from one activity to the next.

Alert: Check all systems before moving. Make sure tanks are full (or empty, as appropriate). Is this child prepared to sit? Does she need a stretch, food, toilet stop?

Resistance: Disengage the brakes by encouraging cooperation. Pull over if things get overheated and motors or tempers need to cool down.

Dethroning:
Cooperation Reigns

Situation: Cooperation Begins with . . .
(Oh No! Not Me — Again!)

A few years ago, while on vacation, we stopped at a family-run store in a rural part of our state. Though officially closed, because we had come so far, the owners opened up for us to shop. They were the kindest family, even inviting us to stay for dinner. My husband, our youngsters, and I had a great visit. What really impressed me were the children in this family. They had two teenage daughters and three elementary-aged sons, all of them incredibly helpful.

While two boys loaded our car with the sacks of grains and other items we had chosen, an older daughter played with our children and handled the transactions at the cash register. When we went inside, one daughter was folding laundry and another son setting the table. Never once did I hear their parents request these children to do anything. There was no squabbling and not a single complaint. However did they achieve that kind of cooperation?

I tried to picture my own children doing anything without being asked, threatened, or coerced. Images of our table set with the silverware tossed in a pile in the middle; laundry gathered with a trail of dirty socks leading down the hall; and worst, of all my usual frantic raving whenever a holiday approached. I decided there was something (or someone?) wrong with our picture. What and how could it be changed?

Solution

With Thanksgiving approaching, our sorry holiday situation seemed like the best place to begin. In years past, one person planned the whole event (alright, let's face facts: I took the role of Queen Mother of Holiday Hosts). I was the one who sent out invitations to friends and relatives, planned the menu, and nagged a royal blue streak trying to get everyone else to help with preparations. I wanted the floors vacuumed, the onions chopped just so, and expected every banner in our kingdom to flap in grandeur from the castle walls.

Alas, my subjects seldom rushed to do my bidding. What Queen Mom got was a cranky group of kids fighting over what television show to watch next. I would ask one child to clean the bathroom and, with luck, he might toss a few towels into the hamper. Another child, sent to clean her bedroom, might manage to cram three stuffed teddy bears and a dirty basketball shirt into her closet. Meanwhile, child number three could be counted on to be whining that her arm was too tired to continue stirring the custard sauce. This level of non-cooperation continued right up to and through the arrival of the guests, by which time Queen Mom's tiara was in serious disarray. As the last guest would cross our moat, all I longed for was my bed, but only after making it plain to all of my offspring that they were grounded for the rest of their lives. ("Off with their heads" sounded appealing, as well.) Holiday cheer? Not here!

STEP ONE: ASK FOR HELP

I considered banning all holidays, but even to my Queenly self, this seemed extreme, so I decided to try something less drastic. Determined to let go of my compulsion to be in charge of everything, I turned to my unwilling brood of peasants and asked for their ideas. This marked a revolutionary step.

First, I told my children that I needed their help. Everyone's ears perked up.

What was mom up to? Was she trying a new, sneaky way to make us do something?

I explained that I hated spoiling the holidays by nagging and yelling at everyone. Wow! Mom was admitting to HER faults! Now they really were listening. I said that I wanted the holidays to be a fun time, but did not know how to make that happen. "Will you help me figure out a better way to do things?" Something really was different. Could this be mom talking?

STEP TWO: LISTEN TO OTHERS

Listening goes both ways. I asked them how they felt about the way we celebrated our holidays. What did they like or not like? One by one they began to talk. I learned that they were uncomfortable when I invited people to holiday events, often people they did not know well, if at all. They wanted to be with their own friends, at least some of the time, and felt constricted by the expectations at home. As we continued to talk — the atmosphere became more open.

STEP THREE: WORK TOGETHER

We talked about what they **did like** and **would like** to have happen on holidays. So, with Thanksgiving in our sights, we began to plan. We made a list of people to invite, their friends included, making sure that each intended guest would be welcomed by all. Next we decided on a menu for the meal and divided up tasks. I not only ended up with cooking helpers but with grocery shopping, serving, and cleaning helpers, too.

The day before the holiday the house was abuzz. One child was waxing the mantle (a task never before even imagined); while another loaded laundry; and a third hoisted the vacuum from room to room. Every one of these tasks was being done — WITHOUT anyone BEING ASKED to do them.

NEW OWNERSHIP

When people feel a sense of ownership,

they care about outcomes.

Smart business people know this. It is true at home as well. The key is that if we want others to cooperate, we need to allow them to feel an investment in the outcome. When children contribute in meaningful ways — from planning, to preparation, to participating in an event — they feel a sense of ownership and care about the results. This had been the secret of that original family with their small store and amazing level of cooperation: *Every family member's efforts had mattered.*

FAREWELL TO THE QUEEN

Our holidays have never been the same since. By asking for help, listening to others, and working together I had managed to usher in a Golden Age of Cooperation for our household. Decades later each of us now has a favorite dinner item to prepare for Thanksgiving dinner and no matter what the holiday or celebration — planning it is a joint effort ensuring that it becomes Our Party — one that everyone can enjoy — together.

Perhaps it is time to consider setting your own royal rule aside. Sooner than you might imagine possible —

Cooperation could reign in your castle, too!

THE MAGIC RECIPE FOR COOPERATION

Ingredients:

1 part — Owning up to your portion of the problem

1 part — Well-ripened and polite request for help

2 (or more) — Dollops of teamwork

Directions:

Add ingredients in the order listed. Stir gently.

Watch as Cooperation's magic rises, filling the air with excited voices, willing hands, and happy hearts.

Enjoy — Together!

#3

Meltdowns —
Frustrations and Tantrums

When the whining doesn't work for your child
and listening isn't working for either or both of you —
someone is going to MELTDOWN.
Next up:
FRUSTRATION and its twin: TANTRUMS.

With so many opportunities for conflict,
*we all **melt-down** at some point.*
Anger is a universal feeling.
Dealing with strong emotions —
our children's and our own —
takes patience, practice, and persistence.

Anger:
Everybody Simmer Down!

Situation: Replacing Red-Hot Reactions with Reasonable Responses

I don't know what to do about my child's anger. She hits me, throws things, and yells whenever she gets upset. She is going to be four next week and I am very anxious to eliminate this anger.

Solution

Anger is a hot topic in more ways than one. We refer to it as **seeing red**, **getting steamed**, and **erupting** — all of which bring to mind images of heat and fire. In truth, anger is a feeling just like sadness, tranquility, or joy. When asked which feeling we would prefer to have, we would be more likely to choose joy than anger; but anger is not really a negative or bad emotion. It is how we **react** to anger that creates problems.

Neither kicking nor yelling will put out a fire.

The truth is, we cannot eliminate anger anymore than we can ban fire. Have you gotten angry this past week? Most everyone does. Anger is not going to disappear. In fact, healthy anger can galvanize us into positive action.

Think of anger as a smoke alarm alerting us to a problem.

MODEL
Children live what they learn. How do you want your child to respond to anger? What did you learn about anger as a child?

"Anger is scary." "Anger is bad." "Anger is dangerous."

What messages are you giving about anger? Is your child learning to handle anger with violence (spanking); that anger is dangerous (yelling and punishment); or that she is responsible for keeping you happy (tears and blame)? Are these the lessons you want to teach?

A child can become angry because he can't have a cookie before lunch. He wants something that is inappropriate, his anger alarm sounds, and life goes on. Just because someone gets angry does not mean that we need to do anything to prevent, fix, or take away that anger. We can empathize and offer comfort:

"You are upset and really want a cookie right now."
"It is hard for you to wait until after dinner."
"Would a hug help?"

LISTEN: TO THE BODY
Anger causes blood to rush to the head submerging the brain beneath a flood of anger chemicals. Our **senses** provide the best drainage system for getting the brain out of flood stage.

Remember the song, "Head and Shoulders" that you sang with your baby? It contains great tips for effective anger responses.

"Eyes, ears, mouth, and nose,
Head and shoulders,
Knees and toes . . . ."

Those words can provide clues for remembering how to obtain cooling relief from overheated emotions. Using the words of the song as our guide — here are ways to handle anger. (Both adults and children will benefit from these techniques.)

COMING TO OUR SENSES: EYES — WINDOWS TO THE SOUL

Use your eyes. Visualize a calm setting: picture a stop sign or look up into the branches of a tree to re-center yourself.

Provide vividly colored felt pens or crayons and encourage your child to draw a picture of her anger as a way to defuse.

EARS — SOOTHING SOUND OR SILENCE

Use your ears. Calming music, a meditation bell, and silence are great tools. Children respond well to quiet spaces too, that is why sending a child to her room can help everyone to cool down.

A soft, soothing voice is much more effective than a loud, shrill response to another's anger.

MOUTH — SIP AND SAVOR

Focus on what goes into your mouth —

to gain control over what ought not come out of it.

Sip a warm drink such as tea or hot cocoa, or a cooling glass of juice to restore your own balance. (This will not be your first response because the digestive system is likely to be shut down in the first flush of anger.)

As the process of calming progresses, a child might enjoy some milk, juice, or warm cocoa, too.

NOSE — BREATHE IN, BLOW OUT

Sniff some flowers, inhale the fragrance of a cup of herbal tea, or just breathe deeply.

Deep breathing is a great skill to teach to children. At a time when no one is angry, demonstrate deep breathing by placing both hands over your chest until your fingertips touch. Then pretend that you are blowing up a balloon and breathe in. Watch your fingertips move apart as your chest expands. Let out your breath and watch your fingertips come back together. Try counting slowly to three or four, for both inhalation and exhalation.

SHOULDERS — TOUCH

Massage your neck, your shoulders, or rub your hands over your face to release anger.

Children do well with a container of play dough to squeeze, flatten, and pound. Splashing in water is also soothing, as is a warm bath or shower. Hugs are great at any age.

KNEES AND TOES — MOVE

Movement releases anger's energy. Go for a walk or run or play a game of chase. For quick relief, try shaking out your arms, legs, and head as you blow out angry energy. Demonstrate this and practice doing it with your child. Maybe she will remind you to try it the next time you start to sizzle!

HEAD — UNDERSTANDING, THE THINKING PART

Using the senses and movement gets the brain out of flood stage. Once the head is available, it becomes possible to think again. Only then is it time to solve the problem that triggered the anger.

What, **Why**, and **How** questions make great problem-solvers. If anger is a smoke alarm — then what caused the smoke?

What happened? Tyler hit Mariana.
Why? "She took my blocks."

This answer signals a lack of skills. Young children need words for their feelings in order to tell others how they feel. They also need to learn how to ask for what they want.

SOLVING PROBLEMS

How else could this problem be handled?

"Hitting Mariana was not okay. Try telling her what you want."
"Those were my blocks. I want them back."

Maybe Mariana will hand them back and maybe not. Wanting something does not mean we get it. Mariana might say, "I want them too. You had them all morning!" At this point more options are needed.

"How can you both play with the same blocks?"

Offer suggestions if children get stuck. "Maybe Mariana can play with them for ten minutes and then Tyler could have them."

Or, "Perhaps you could build something together."

Finding new possibilities is the key to successful problem-solving. It is vital to the problem-solving process to recognize that there are many possibilities — beyond the two extremes of: either **my way** or **your way**.

PRACTICE, PRACTICE, PRACTICE

Practice skills when no one is angry.

"Show me how you can take deep breaths when you need to calm down."
"When you are angry at your sister, where is the play dough that you can use to help get your anger out?"
"How could you tell your friend that you want to play with her tricycle?"

This combination approach of Coming to our Senses; Learning from our Anger; and Solving Problems won't eradicate anger, but it will provide healthy ways in which to respond to anger, and prevent emotional flare-ups from raging out of control.

TAKE IT FROM THE TOP!

Eyes, ears, mouth, and nose,
Head and shoulders,
Knees and toes . . . .

Simmer down. Come to your senses.
Undercover the **What**, **Why**, and **How** that trigger anger's alarms.
Problem-solve with cool heads.
Practice these three steps: **before**, **during**, and **after** anger erupts.

Throwing Tantrums:
Yours and Theirs

Situation: Tantrums are for Kids

I am having a problem with my four-year-old son. He loves to play at his friend's house or have his friend over to play. The problem is that he throws a complete fit when he has to leave his friend's house, or it is time for his friend to leave our house. He yells, kicks, and throws himself to the ground. I end up carrying him off screaming (me as well as him!).

It seems when he is told "No" for whatever reason, he gets mad; stomps his feet; and yells, throwing a huge tantrum. I have tried to reason with him, but it doesn't seem to be working. How can we avoid these outbursts?

Solution

Your son does not want to quit playing, leave his friend's house, or have his friend leave his house. The word "No" almost guarantees a struggle. In other words, no matter what you do your son may still throw a tantrum. Avoiding his tantrum is less important than managing to avoid throwing one of your own. There are things that will help both of you. Practice preventive parenting; say "No" less often; and find ways to seek cooperation. Here's how.

PRACTICE PREVENTIVE PARENTING

- **Plan ahead.** Before allowing your son to go to his friend's house, discuss expectations for leaving. Talk these through.
- **Involve him in the planning.** Ask him what needs to happen when you say it is time to leave.
- **Clarify expectations.** Tell him what you will do when it is time to leave: "I will gather up our things and tell you it is time to leave. You may hold my hand or I will carry you."
- **Check it out.** Ask him to repeat what needs to happen when it is time to leave. "We hold hands to go to the car." Congratulate him on responding accurately. He will enjoy feeling competent.
- **Do what you say you will do.** When time is up, gather up coats, shoes, and his toy fire truck. Tell him it is time to leave. If he refuses, offer to hold his hand or carry him. If he resists, carry him. Stay calm.

It is respectful to both of you to follow-through on what is said.

At least only one of you will be screaming!

- **Discuss unacceptable behavior.** Ask him what things are not okay to do if he doesn't want to leave (i.e., kicking, hitting, and screaming). Continue asking him questions (resist telling him the answers), thus allowing him to feel empowered. Giving appropriate power is the opposite of a power struggle.
- **Practice.** Role-play leaving his friend's with each of you taking a turn in the role of parent and child. Act out both appropriate and inappropriate behavior. Children usually find doing this (especially the misbehaving part) great fun.
- **Devise a private signal.** Decide upon a signal to indicate that it is time to leave: humming a song; a big wink; or tugging at your earlobe. Exaggerate and be silly!

SAY "NO" LESS OFTEN

A big key to changing your son's pattern of defiance and resistance is to learn to say "No" less often. When we examine most situations, the need to say "No" often evaporates.

- **Qualify your "Yes" response.** If your son asks for a cookie, instead of an abrupt "No!" try: "You may have a cookie right after lunch."

- **Anticipate problems.** A summons to leave the playground might meet with a request for "Just one more time on the swing." Instead of responding with "No" after the fact — go back to prevention.

  Before saying it is time to go, ask him what toys he wants to play on before leaving. He lists them off and you agree to his plans, explaining that he has ten more minutes left to fit in those activities. Ask if he needs a one or two minute warning before time is up.

- **Empower with limited choices.** Before entering the grocery store, offer your child choices. "You may choose between juice, cookies, or fruit for today's treat." This works much better than having to say "No" to the bubble gum, soda pop, and candy he begs to have.

  Limited choices include only acceptable alternatives.

SEEK SOLUTIONS

The word "No" is really only part of the problem. The broader issue involves a power struggle. Stop focusing on what you are **trying** to make him do or not do. Learn to empower yourself and your child — instead of battling for control.

- **Claim the problem as your own.**
  "I really don't like carrying you home after visits next door. I want to figure out a better way of ending play time and coming home."

- **Ask for your son's help with the problem.** "Would you be willing to help me come up with a plan for solving this problem?"

- **Invite thinking.** Ask questions. "I've noticed how upset we both get when it is time to quit playing. What can we do about this problem?"

This invites your child to be part of the solution, respects his ability to solve problems, and encourages him to change his behavior.

Prevention is always easier than solving problems.

Children learn respectful behavior

by experiencing it.

- **Listen and share ideas.** Agree upon a plan that works for both of you. Children often come up with brilliant, unexpected, and creative solutions. If your son won't choose a solution, choose one and ask him to agree to try it for the next week.

Most children are willing to agree to a short trial period.

LEAVE TANTRUMS TO THEM

As to your son's tantrums, quit worrying. He can choose to have a tantrum or not. Avoiding children's tantrums is not the goal of parenting. Sometimes young children just want things their way (don't we all?) and they are much less inhibited about letting the world know about it.

Allow him to have his tantrum, making sure he is in a safe place when he does so (away from sharp table corners, hard surfaces, or tippy furniture). Try to remain calm and give the tantrum as little attention as possible.

More importantly, do not throw your own tantrum. Breathe. Stay kind.

Remember:

Tantrums are temporary.

#4

Negotiation and Manipulation

We say, "It's time for bed."
Little Agatha says, "I'm not sleepy."
We say, "No treats."
Young Rosa holds up a cookie, pleading for "Just one more"
as her tear-filled eyes threaten to overflow. . . .
We read one story and Abraham says,
"Daddy always reads me three. . . . "
Exactly when does negotiation stop —
and manipulation begin?
Let's see how desperate or clever they —
and we — can get.

The Store:
Grocery Store Grief

Situation: Shopping in Public

Every time I go to the grocery store my daughter pitches a fit in the checkout line. She sees all the candy and toys and if I refuse to buy her one she starts screaming, kicking, and hitting me.

I often buy her something just to get out of the store, save face, and quiet her down. Other times I stand firm but end up spanking her. Either way I feel awful.

Solution:

The responses you describe have the potential to teach your daughter some powerful lessons. These are three of them. She might learn that:

- The way to get what she wants is to make a scene.
- She need not wait for what she wants.
- Other people are totally unpredictable.

SCENE-MAKERS

Her eventual mate, teachers, and co-workers won't appreciate lesson #1. Imagine a future social gathering. Her spouse is bold enough to suggest they leave early while she is still having a wonderful time.

She says, "Stay!" He says, "Go!"

Uh-oh!

NOW!

Lesson #2 is no less promising. It makes the prospect of a credit card in her hands truly horrific. She thinks, "I want that dress — I'll get that dress." "Charge it, please," rolls off her tongue with practiced ease.

PREDICTABILITY AND TRUST

Lastly, why bother to learn to tell others how she feels about problems if lesson #3 holds true? Lesson #3 teaches that people are unpredictable. A friend promising to go shopping; a teacher announcing that late papers won't be accepted; or the life insurance cancellation notice stating that payment must be received within the next two weeks — none of these mean much. Why believe these things will or won't happen if others cannot be trusted to do what they say?

Unpredictability weakens one's ability to trust.

SHORT TERM RESULTS

It is doubtful you want to teach your child these life lessons, and it can be easy to give in to the temptation of short-term results, but today's candy bar will only stop today's tantrum. The best time to deal with your daughter's behavior is before you even enter the store.

GOOD-BYE GRIEF

Compare the strategies in the following chart to your present repeated battles at the checkout stand. Consider the extra time involved as a long-term investment in both of your futures. The only loss is going to be that large bag of **grocery grief** you've been stockpiling daily.

GRIEF-PROOF SHOPPING

Talk over expectations before going into the store. "I need to get milk for breakfast and a loaf of bread. Then I want to pay and leave the store quickly." This gives your child a clear picture of the shopping trip.

Ask for her help. Involve her. "Will you help me remember what we need to buy?" "Would you like to choose the bread and carry it for me?"

Solve problems in advance using questions. "What if you see something you really want, like a candy bar? Is a candy bar on our list?" This last question opens up an opportunity for the two of you to avoid a future conflict.

Plan ahead. Be prepared with several options if problems do arise. If she asks for an item not agreed upon in advance:

- Offer to help her write it on a list to consider buying next time.

- Assist her in figuring out how many weeks' allowance it will take for her to buy it herself.

Both of these teach **delayed gratification** and help to discourage impulsivity.

Give her a specific amount of money to spend on an item she might want. (This is best with children from late four and older. It is also a great way to introduce children to handling money.)

- Do NOT increase the agreed upon spending amount if the item costs more. Commiserate with her that it is too expensive.

- Help her figure out ways to save up for or earn enough to buy an item. (Perhaps offer to match what she saves if the item is pricey.)

- **Set boundaries in advance.** Do NOT place limits on what she can buy **after** you are in the store. Try:

  "You may buy juice, chocolate milk, or cookies."
  "You may not buy candy."

  These steps temper impulsivity with reality.

  Explain what _you_ will do if a problem occurs at the store and **follow-through** on what you say. "I've decided that if there is any kicking, yelling, or hitting — we will need to leave the store at once."

- She kicks. You both leave. That's being predictable!

- It is wise to plan a trip to the store at a time when you can follow-through by leaving in the middle of your shopping, since most children will check to see if you really meant what you said.

- Be prepared to abandon that grocery basket, frozen juice and all, as you carry a raging child out with you. (No one ever said being a parent was an ego boost! The key is to avoid beginning your own tantrum.) By doing what we say we will do — we become predictable. Predictability promotes trust.

  TIP: Following-through sounds inconvenient, embarrassing, and exhausting. In fact, it is — but living with a tyrant is worse, and it is rare that you will need to follow all-the-way through more than once or twice, because (trust me) each time is sure to be memorable.

"I Want It!"
Untangling the Tentacles
of Commercialism

Situation: "I want it!" Untangling the Tentacles of Commercialism

Any time my child sees a new princess doll advertised on television, a cartoon-related display at the mall, or a cereal box picturing a favorite movie character — she wants it. I hate to say, "No" to everything but it doesn't feel right to me to pay more for a box of cereal or a toy because of a pink princess on the package. Any suggestions?

Solution: Who Really Cares about Your Child?

The tentacles of commercialism, like an omnipresent octopus from cyberspace entwine us all and our children are a particularly tempting tidbit. Unless you have tucked your family away on a remote mountaintop or in a cave, the media will find you (although I suppose the cave could be outfitted with a satellite dish . . .).

Children absorb what they see and hear. I remember asking one little girl what a new movie that was being advertised was about. She said, "Coming to a theater near you." I found that answer scary — don't you?

She says, "Stay!" He says, "Go!"

Uh-oh!

NOW!

Lesson #2 is no less promising. It makes the prospect of a credit card in her hands truly horrific. She thinks, "I want that dress — I'll get that dress." "Charge it, please," rolls off her tongue with practiced ease.

PREDICTABILITY AND TRUST

Lastly, why bother to learn to tell others how she feels about problems if lesson #3 holds true? Lesson #3 teaches that people are unpredictable. A friend promising to go shopping; a teacher announcing that late papers won't be accepted; or the life insurance cancellation notice stating that payment must be received within the next two weeks — none of these mean much. Why believe these things will or won't happen if others cannot be trusted to do what they say?

Unpredictability weakens one's ability to trust.

SHORT-TERM RESULTS

It is doubtful you want to teach your child these life lessons, and it can be easy to give in to the temptation of short-term results, but today's candy bar will only stop today's tantrum. The best time to deal with your daughter's behavior is before you even enter the store.

GOOD-BYE GRIEF

Compare the strategies in the following chart to your present repeated battles at the checkout stand. Consider the extra time involved as a long-term investment in both of your futures. The only loss is going to be that large bag of **grocery grief** you've been stockpiling daily.

The truth is that it isn't just the kids who are tempted by those cute, fur-trimmed pixie cute slippers, shiny princess lunchboxes, and well, surely a few bowls of double-gunk cereal can't be all that bad . . . right? What about the designer slacks, sports hero athletic shoes, or brand name beer or beauty creams that fill the halls and cabinets of our homes? We are in the unique position of being both part of the problem (because commercialism affects us, too), as well as the ones whose job is it to protect our children from exploitation. This is a little-appreciated role; in fact, it feels more like being designated the vice squad officer of fairyland. An adult's "No" is often the precursor to a child's meltdown at the mall, in the aisles of the grocery store, or under the dining room table with all the relatives looking on. Does it require pointing out that this may not be fun?

WHY WE WANT IT

We all want things — and advertisers are good at their jobs. When we regard something as scarce (or in market terms **unique**) we find it desirable. That is what branding (such as cartoon character or label identification) is all about. In his article "Out of Time" (Winter 2006, Yes! magazine) Jonathan Rowe describes this as **psychologically induced scarcity**. We want what we lack, and we perceive something as lacking when it is seen as scarce, special, or unique. The result is, "I want it", and it isn't just our kids.

Of course we're going to succumb to advertising's lure from time to time, and even if we could manage to resist those pleas from our sweet, round-eyed children, there would still be Grandma Fran, Auntie Alice, and Uncle Joe for them to charm. What can we do? Well actually, quite a lot.

INVITE THINKING

Among the many products used to entice children are foods. Targeted items often contain high levels of sugar and/or fat and lack nutrients. Research has now linked advertising that targets children to the growth of obesity in youngsters twelve and under. This is no longer simply speculation.

Invite your child to think about what he eats. Ask your son what makes that particular (double-fat chemical-laden) cookie so yummy? Then ask him what you and he put into the bowl when you make cookies. "Flour. Eggs. Sugar."

Now read the ingredients on Amazing Spiderman® or Little Nemo® fruit-flavored snacks. "Hmm. Does carnauba wax sound like something we want to eat? What do you think sulfiting agents taste like?" Learning to check ingredients is a great habit — for everyone. This kind of awareness invites children to become critical consumers, who will question and think about their world.

What if you said, "Why don't we make cookies tonight after dinner?" Wow, not only would he get cookies with real ingredients, but the two of you could also share time together. That's a double-filled deal — no doubt about it.

Here is another approach. Compare how many boxes of Creepy Flakes a certain amount of money (say $5) will buy. This won't work with children younger than six or even seven, as money and its value are still difficult concepts for them, but as they grow older, children can become aware of the real value of what they (or you) get for that package price.

Both of these approaches involve children in thinking and aren't thinking kids what we really want? By just saying "No" or telling a child that a product is "not good" or "overpriced", we leave the door open to rebellion or power struggles. None of us learned to think without opportunities to practice.

Encouraging thinking is thoughtful parenting in action.

PREVENTION PAYS OFF

Another way to resist commercialism is to inoculate against it. Spend time watching television with your child. Notice what is being advertised. Ask your child why she thinks this (toy, food, or game) would be fun to have. Listen to her answers. Ask questions. Share your thoughts. This listening/sharing process encourages thinking and provides "Aha!" moments (for both of you).

When the two of you see or hear things that you don't like — talk over what you could do about it. Work together to write a letter to a toy company, food manufacturer, or restaurant chain. Tell them what you don't like about a flimsy doll, a sugar-laden cereal, or the lack of fruit or milk in their children's menu. You will be heard (businesses consider every written complaint to be representative of many more). You will also be teaching your child to see herself as capable, empowered, and able to effect change in her world. These are fabulous life skills that are crucial to a child's self-esteem. Such experiences build resilience that will show up whenever she faces adversity of any kind.

What a grand seven-league jump from feeling like a grump for saying "No" — to helping your child make positive and meaningful contributions in the world and feeling empowered to do so. This has to be a way better deal than anything super-sized at the local eatery.

YOUR ACTIONS

We also make statements through our actions. Every time we do not buy an item that exploits children or treats them as a target for profit, we have performed an action that will resonate at the cash registers.*

As with a mosquito's bite — even a tiny sting gets felt.

WATCH WHAT THEY WATCH

Prevention is always easier than solving problems. At times there are so many toys, trinkets, and branded products available for an upcoming movie that we have to wonder if the paraphernalia was meant to advertise the movie, or the other way around (in fact, it often is!). Instead, support programming that does not market to children. Public television provides such programming and your money can be spent to support them through donations, instead of additional purchases.

Other options are to switch off the television set or tame its influence with technology. Access a service that will record programs (deleting the commercials) for later viewing. Either option puts you back in control of what your child is exposed to.

The library has great alternatives to commercial programming. There are many children's videos available, often with animated versions of children's storybook classics or folktales, which can be enjoyed over and over.

Discover the many advertising-free children's magazines available. These publications are full of craft projects, puzzles, and recipes that invite creativity, exploration, and learning and are available for infants through teens. Check some out at your local library to find ones you and your child enjoy, and then subscribe to your favorites.

You may not have to resort to excavating a cave in which to raise your children; but it may take serious digging, along with plenty of thought and action — both yours and theirs — to evade commercialism's tempting tentacles.

*Note: Campaign for a Commercial-Free Childhood (CCFC) offers many additional ways to act on children's behalf.
Their web site is: www.commercialfreechildhood.org.

ROSLYN'S TIMELESS
NON-COMMERCIAL BIRTHDAY GIFT GUIDE

UNDER AGE 2:
- Crayons or pens that only work on special paper (no mess on floors, tables, or other surfaces)
- Large soft balls
- Clear balls with moving objects inside

AGE 2:
- Soft puzzles
- Wooden puzzles with knobs
- Bath toys (plastic funnels and unbreakable measuring cups for pouring)

AGE 3:
- Basket filled with 1/2 yard pieces of fabric (glittery/silky/lacy/ethnic prints)
- Flashlight (duct tape battery holder closed or buy one that has to be opened with a screwdriver; do not get LED lit ones, which can be harmful to eyes)
- Muffin pan, fancy cupcake papers, wooden spoon, and cake mix
- Bubble-blowing supplies

AGE 4:
- Binoculars
- Magnifying glass
- Dress up items: selection of gowns, vests, scarves, gloves, etc. (thrift stores and yard sales are great sources); place these in a special basket, large hatbox, or fancy box
- Dress up hats: cowboy, hardhats, firemen helmets, veils, and captain's hats
- Small garden tools, seed packets, planting containers

ROSLYN'S TIMELESS
NON-COMMERCIAL BIRTHDAY GIFT GUIDE

AGE 5:
- Crayons with interesting templates (textured surfaces and patterns, natural designs like leaves or tree bark, a selection of embossed holiday cards)
- Ice cream or popsicle maker (with recipes)
- Bike helmet
- Disposable camera
- Card games
- Bird feeder

AGE 6 AND UP:
- Hula hoop
- Jump rope
- Craft supplies of all kinds
- Large knitting needles, crochet hook, yarn (and a certificate to teach how to use them)

FOR ALL AGES:
- Books/art supplies (vary by age)
- Music
- Any offer of time (feeding ducks, trip to the zoo, tickets to a play, the circus, or a children's museum)

FAVORITE PARTY TIP:
- Wrap a box in multiple layers of paper. Pass it around for all children to unwrap, layer by layer; inside are small party favors (raisins, magnifiers, bubble-blowing supplies)

This shared unwrapping takes the boredom and sting out of the birthday person getting ALL the attention (and all the loot!).

They Do It Differently: Different Rules/Different People/ Different Ways

Situation: They Do It Differently: Different Rules/ Different People/Different Ways

When our son's friends visit, I often find myself defending how we do things. If I say we take off our shoes inside — one of the children will announce, "We don't do that at our house." If I offer to make sandwiches, another child will say, "That's not the kind of bread we eat." Today someone asked me where we kept our recycling can. When I said, "We don't have one," he said, "But then you're killing trees." Yikes! I am tired of explaining that we do things differently and I don't like feeling that I have to defend our choices." I don't think our rules are unreasonable, but often I feel like the wicked witch for having to constantly announce and enforce them.

Solution: Our Way — Not Everyone's

Children assume that the way things are done at their house — is the way things are done, period. Instead of feeling defensive as each difference gets highlighted — recognize that your differences are helping this child to broaden his view of the world. Your rules reflect what works for your family. Children aren't sitting in judgment of you, but learning about the world outside their doors — and in so doing, defining their own world, as well.

As to feeling like a wicked witch, get over it. Before you are through raising your child, there will surely be a far worse thing you're accused of being and you may well find yourself looking back upon **wicked witch** as one of your kinder personae.

RESISTANCE AND INSISTENCE

We all have a tendency to like things that are familiar, seeking ways to maintain our own personal status quo. This could explain the motivation behind a child's comments. It seems to be human nature to resist change.

On the other hand, when a child says that something is or is not done at **our house** it may simply be shorthand for saying, "I want to do it my way." Either approach, whether resistance or insistence, provides an opportunity for a lesson in mutual respect.

"Yes, you have a different rule at your house. But when you play at our house, we have our rules to follow." The triple message that comes through is: differences are okay; rules change; and either way, we need to respect the rules — wherever we are.

WHY CAN'T WE . . .

On the flip side of defending **your way** to the neighbor's children is defending it to your own.

"At Becky's house they always have cookies and popsicles. All we ever have are apples."
"Billy watches cartoons anytime he wants. How come I never get to?"
"Teema's mom lets her wear eye shadow for Halloween. Please mommy — I want pink sparkles."

As your children grow older, you will be amazed at how such statements will begin to describe ever more bizarre behaviors that **everyone** else has, gets to do, or is not restricted from doing. It is also interesting that whatever situation is described is usually portrayed in extremes such as: **all**; **never**; or **anytime he wants**.

Of course, it may be true that one hot day three months ago Becky's mom did serve your child frozen juice on a stick and perhaps six months ago there was a plate of cookies on their countertop. But there is an even better chance that this gilded memory of **always** stems more from dissatisfaction with today's apple slices than from any real-life cornucopia of cookies and popsicles in another household.

Don't defend — agree. There is a difference. "They do it differently." Billy may be permitted to watch cartoons 24/7 and maybe one day he will rival Disney's fame with his own cartoon channel — but, "In our house getting dressed, eating breakfast, and brushing teeth are the way mornings begin."

"You would really like to wear eye shadow and someday you will." We can acknowledge what a child is asking for without granting it, while we reassure her that someday what she wants may be possible. Follow up with a choice that is acceptable. "Look at the super sparkly pink necklaces I got for you to wear." Your rules are different — and you need to honor them if you want anyone else to do so. Acknowledge, commiserate, and then — do it your way (which is of course 'our way' since you and your child share the same home and rules).

PREVENTION AND GUIDANCE
Children are capable of adjusting to different expectations with amazing agility. Thea Alexandria might condone jumping on the bed but little Dimitri knows that Mama does not. At Papa's house it may be fine to start the day with a slice of leftover pizza, but Grandma says, "No leftovers for breakfast. We have milk or juice in the morning." It really doesn't matter what the rules are — children understand that rules are different and will adapt.

Of course, we all forget (or pretend to forget) things, especially if we don't care for a particular rule. Lila needs reminders to eat her crackers at the table when she visits her great-grandma at the nursing home. She may forget this rule, or simply not want to sit still long enough to finish her snack. It always helps to go over special rules in advance of arrival at a different place or event. The best way to do this is to ask questions. "Can you remember where you are allowed to eat when we visit Granny?" Questions keep children engaged in the process — something a droning lecture fails to do: "Now, remember, at Grammy's you must eat only at blah, blah, blah. . . ." Snore. Lectures work better than lullabies at putting a mind into snooze mode.

FLEXIBILITY IS AN ASSET
There are lots of different rules out there. We can run and scream at the park but not in the mosque. We can walk into the bathroom when mom is in the shower — but not when a houseguest is bathing. We can slide down the stair banister at home but not at school or run through the hall at Uncle Juan's but not at the public library. The list is infinite. Teaching children that things are done differently — in all kinds of situations, is teaching them about the real world. Differences are facts of life and 'our way' is not the 'only' or 'right' way of doing things. This is a lesson with big implications.

FROM DEFENSE TO DELIGHT
Instead of defending your lack of a recycling bin (something it wouldn't hurt you to consider, by the way), smile and say, "We don't have one. Isn't it interesting that things are different at different houses?" This invites children to see differences as worth exploring — and piques their curiosity. We do it different — how about that? Wow! Since the world is filled with lots of differences, **wow** is a great life-attitude, and when coupled with mutual respect, it may even be the key to world peace.

RISK-TAKING
Wouldn't it get boring if everything were the same every place we went? Yes — and no. We like the comfort of familiarity, something fast food and chain stores capitalize upon. But when we encourage children to see **new** and **different** as worthwhile and worthy of respect, we give them a priceless gift and open them to a world of exploration. Discovering differences is an awesome lifelong adventure. Doing things only one way — **our way** — fences us in and limits the life we experience. When we step outside our doors — the differences we encounter enrich us. Yes — others do it differently, and aren't we lucky they do? Differences give life texture, while mutual respect for those differences transforms our living into a rich tapestry of experience.

#5 to #8

The Top Ten Preschool Parenting Problems

*Now we come to the most crowded section
of this book. Problems #5 through #8
may not have the tortuous intensity of the first 4,
but they sure can wear us down.
These next problems are those daily things
we slog through, from getting up in the morning,
through brushing teeth and bolting down bagels,
to diaper duty and bath or bedtime battles — 24/7.*

#5a

Morning Hassles

Go. Go. Go.
Hurry. Hurry. Hurry.
No! No! No!
And, thus, the day begins . . .

Getting Dressed

Situation: From Morning Combat to Life Skills

John is wearing a polar fleece pullover, wool slacks, and heavy socks with boots.
His four-year-old daughter, Chelsea, looks like an ad for a Hawaiian vacation.
Even the mention of pants, a sweatshirt, or (horrors) her coat causes an outcry.
Today Chelsea dressed herself in a lacy skirt topped by a flowered yellow top with
her summer sandals completing the outfit. There is snow on the ground, and
Chelsea's coat is lying on the floor between them like a battle banner.

Solution

Sometimes the amount of clothing a child has on is a good indication of how
cold the accompanying adult is. Of course, snow on the ground versus summer
sandals does not sound like this adult is overstating the need for a coat, but
children above the age of two-and-a-half are usually well able to maintain their
body heat.

One good measure of whether a child is dressed warmly enough is to feel her
hands. An active child will have warm hands on even the coldest day. Sometimes
that same child will be wearing only a sweater, a light jacket, or have her heavy

coat unbuttoned. Meanwhile, the adults in the nearby vicinity look like they are going to scale Mt. Everest in a blizzard. People have differing needs.

The real need is to help children learn to make sensible choices.

MEANINGFUL EXPERIENCE

Rather than battle over what to wear, or if she needs a coat or not, help her learn to make appropriate choices. Children need safe ways in which to experience life. A child bundled up to his eyebrows as sparrows trill in the apple blossoms overhead won't know what **cold** means. Even more to the point, young children do not understand that **feeling cold** and **wearing certain types of clothing** (or not) relate to one another. Of course, adults **tell** children about coats, clothing, and warmth, but this is not the same as **experiencing** warmth, cold, or the relationship of clothing to body temperature.

Imagine that you had never seen a lemon before. Others warned you that lemons are **sour**, but you have no experience of **sour**. You are hungry and see a slice of lemon. Until you bite into it, pucker up, and squint at the taste, you won't understand what **sour** means, but the next time you see a lemon you will be much less likely to sink your teeth into it because **sour** is now a concept you have experienced.

MAKING CONNECTIONS

Back to the cold winter day. What does it feel like to be cold? Does what a person wear make a difference? Let your daughter head outside in her sundress, sandals, and lacy clothes. Simply put her warm clothes, socks, and coat in the car. She will start to notice her discomfort. Instead of telling her why she is getting uncomfortable, ask her to describe her problem. She might respond that her arms have bumps on them.

Give her information and continue to ask questions instead of telling her all the answers. "Those sound like goose bumps. What do you suppose causes goose bumps?" She might surprise you and say that her arms have goose bumps because she forgot to eat her toast.

Children interpret experiences differently.

This is a great opportunity for you to help her learn some new connections. Agree that eating toast is a very good idea, but that it probably is not the reason she has goosebumps on her arms.

Keep talking this through. Point out that she is not wearing a coat. Does she think a coat might make a difference? Comment that, "I think you will feel much more comfortable with your coat on. Coats help our bodies keep warm."

Then encourage her cooperation. "Your coat is on the seat. Do you need help getting it on?" This gives her the chance to feel that wearing the coat is her decision (an important distinction if power struggles are common to a relationship).

LIFE SKILLS VERSUS CHILLS

When adults invite children to learn life skills, children learn to make sound choices. Next time you are ready to leave, ask your child what the weather looks like. If it is cold out, ask what she will need to wear to keep warm. She may still announce that she wants her summer dress. While she is learning to improve her choices, calmly include the coat in the supplies you gather for an outing.

If a child does not begin to make more appropriate choices, perhaps it is time to make some changes. Store the summer dresses until the weather warms up, or the next time you leave home, **don't** pack the coat. Do this on a short trip when she can safely experience the natural outcome of her decision. (Do not leave the coat behind when heading out for an all-day hike in the snow; that would be unsafe. Natural consequences need to be safe and reasonable.)

When she becomes uncomfortable, commiserate with her. Ask, don't tell, her why she may be feeling uncomfortable and what she might have done to prevent being cold. This way you can still congratulate her on being clever enough to figure out the solution to her problem — which is that she ought to have worn her coat, even as she shivers beside you. This is not heartless, even though it may feel that way.

Assure her that you are confident she will remember her coat next time, then head inside to warm up, even it if means canceling the current outing.

The following day, as you prepare to go out — show faith and trust her. "What do you need to wear?" She will remember (trust me).

HINTS FOR MORNING SUCCESS

- Expect that everyone be dressed before eating breakfast (much easier than complicated timing systems).
- Consider no television on in the mornings (simpler than disengaging from a program in progress).
- Alternately, the television only goes on after certain tasks (eating, getting dressed, or tooth brushing) take place.
- Eliminate most morning decision-making:
  — Choose clothes the night before.
  — Plan breakfast menus on a weekly basis (or at least the previous night).
  — Gather needed supplies in advance (coats, shoes, lunch boxes, water bottles) and place them in a designated spot.
- Involve everyone. Even young children can set out silverware, carry fruit to the table, or load their cereal bowls into the dishwasher.

Contribution creates belonging.

- Decide what you will do when the morning runs ragged (instead of what you will make, or try to make, your child do). Tell your child what to expect:
  — I will turn off the television if it is on when it should not be. (Then DO IT!)
  — I will place shoes or jackets in the car if they are not on when it is time to leave. (DO SO — without comment.)
- I will put breakfast things away at (a specific time).

Tip: Set a timer.

REMEMBER — This morning began last night. Are you prepared? Are you organized? Are you both well rested?

HAVE A GREAT DAY!

To Child Care We Go: Stay-at-Home or Child Care? Guilt to Spare

Situation: Working Mom's Guilt

Ever since I've gone back to work, I feel awful about leaving my son at child care. People say that it is wrong for mothers to be away from their children and I feel so guilty, but it is impossible for me to quit my job. I want to do what is best for my son, but feel confused by all the negative things people say about child care. Am I a bad mom?

Solution

Mothers feel guilty leaving young children in child care; others criticize their choices; and all parents worry about doing what is in their children's best interests. Bringing your son to child care does not make you a bad mom.

The issue is less about from whom or where a child receives care, but more about the quality of that care — whatever it is; yet judgmental opinions abound.

WORK, WOMEN, AND CHILD CARE

What is a **working mom**? Chu-Lan dispenses prescriptions from the pharmacy at the corner grocery store. Her four year old attends Little Gifts Child Care for eight hours each day. She fits today's definition of a **working mom**.

So how do we define Marie? Marie stays home with fourteen-month-old Susie and four-year-old Jeff. On Mondays she brings the children to a nursery at the gym while she takes an exercise class. On Tuesdays, Marie volunteers at her church, helping with office tasks while her little ones attend playgroup in the church basement. Every other Wednesday she trades babysitting with a neighbor so she can help assemble the weekly bulletin at her older daughter's elementary school.

Sounds like **work** to me. A **working mom** is a woman who **works**, whether inside or outside of the home, for pay or not.

CHILD CARE

Then what do we mean by **child care**? Is it being in the care of someone besides mom? The church playgroup would fit this definition, as does the gym nursery and the babysitting trade.

Somehow the terms **working mom** and **child care** have narrowed to include only women working **regular** jobs while their children spend time in child care centers or daycare homes. This narrowed definition paints a false nostalgic picture of mothers, children, and childrearing.

EXTENDED FAMILY

Extended family members are the traditional source of shared childrearing worldwide. In Singapore, grandparents are seen as such an integral part of the extended family structure that if their children fail to provide for them in their old age, the government will deduct the cost of an aging parent's care from his or her children's resources — a pretty strong cultural message.

Muslim families in Dubai expect a son's family to move into the ancestral home where grandparents and aunts and uncles will share the care of children.

In many parts of Africa and elsewhere, children have traditionally taken responsibility for younger siblings while mothers and fathers work, whether that work is tilling a family garden or sorting parts in a factory.

When viewed from this perspective, the task of caring for young children (a.k.a. child care) is not, nor has it ever been, a one-on-one mother and child-only arrangement. The key difference is that these caregivers were more often related (i.e., extended family members).

FAMILY WORK — WITHOUT A COMMUTE

Another factor has changed childrearing, and that is where work takes place. Family work had traditionally been done at or from the home and with telecommuting, as well as home businesses, it is still done from home in many places today. But there is a difference. The work itself may no longer be quite as family-friendly.

Today, as in the past, a restaurant in Puerto Vallarta is set up in the front of the family's home, where guests enjoy homemade cinnamon toast, while the family's children eat oranges at the next table under their parents' watchful eyes. This atmosphere is child-welcoming and common in many countries.

Years ago, typical Vietnamese produce stands situated on the family front porch were also common. Children chatted with customers, bagged tender, fresh-picked greens, and learned to weigh rice as part of a normal day. This, too, had been an easy means of blending work and family life.

In America, 'mom and pop' stores once proliferated. Families lived upstairs over a drugstore, deli, or market and children played behind the counter as mom and dad served customers. I can remember many wonderful meals shared in the back room of a neighbor's shoe repair shop or helping my grandfather choose broccoli and bananas at a classmate's family fruit and vegetable market. Work and home intertwined. Parents **worked** and children were **cared** for — all in the same place.

But today's parent working at home is more likely to be sitting at a computer — something that requires concentration and does not offer much social interaction or child-friendly tasks in which little ones can engage. It may be easier to pop in a load of laundry or start a pot of soup cooking, but unless you can limit worktime to naptime, telecommuting is not the same as **being home**. When today's parents make their homes into workplaces, the children will need tending and that means outside child care or a separate caregiver available in the home.

These, and other changes across the globe, mean that who does child care and where it takes place has changed or is changing.

REINVENTING THE PAST

Extended family members are absent from many lives today. The workplace has moved across town or across continents. Children leave home to go to college, take jobs, or migrate from rural to urban locations. Grandparents may be on business trips of their own. Holiday travelers queue at baggage claim kiosks or rely on hand-held cell phones rather than real hands to connect to those they love. Who or what can replace or at least stand-in for absent family members or be there while parents commute to and from distant workplaces?

Today's child care programs often do. A teacher may have to substitute for Aunt Flossy when advice about little Julie's thumb sucking is needed. A child care director may become the one to dispense granny-like comfort to a new parent worried about a child's picky eating habits. Child care centers are places to meet other parents and find connections when family and friends are far away, when the going gets rough, or when a half continent may separate us from one another.

IT TAKES A VILLAGE . . .

The support and care of young children and their families requires a community. It always has. Working parents feel guilty; stay-at-home moms feel defensive; and both feel overwhelmed. Such attitudes do not bring serenity or joy to anyone, and judgmental attitudes isolate us from one another.

The truth is: we are all in this — together.

CHOICES ARE DIFFERENT — NOT GOOD OR BAD

Marilyn, divorced since her daughter turned eight months old, receives no child support from her now unemployed ex-husband. Raising her child alone forces her to make tough choices. She works and her child attends child care.

Dr. Jo returned to her oncology practice when her daughter turned six months old. She trained for 12 years to become a doctor and saves hundreds of lives each year. She believes her ability to offer healing is a special gift, which she feels an obligation to honor. Her daughter thrives at a nearby infant and toddler center. More than financial choice can influence one's decisions.

Maya takes care of her three children at home. They live on her husband, Juan's, safety technician's salary. Her children watch Maya as she works around the house, solicits contributions from neighbors for the local cancer center, or prepares the garden for planting. The loss of the income from her former bank teller's position makes money tight, but staying home while her children were young was Maya's first priority, one she and Juan were able to make a reality.

EXAMINE YOUR CHOICES

Examine your choices. Does your family need the income you can provide? Are you a happier, more productive person when involved in your job? Does doing your work give your child a nicer mom to be around, even if the time together adds up to fewer hours overall?

Perhaps job sharing or **flextime**, where you share a position with someone in order to work fewer hours each day, or to have more control over your working hours so that you may alternate child care responsibilities with a spouse, housemate, or neighbor is a possibility. The son of a night nurse could sleep at a neighbor's house. She could reciprocate by picking up the neighbor's children after school and watching them in the afternoons until their parents got home. These are examples of ways to reduce the need for outside child care facilities; but whatever choices you make, be sure that safety and quality top the list.

If working outside the home is the right choice for you and your situation, then apply your energy to finding **quality** care for your child — instead of wasting it on unproductive guilt. Guilt is a choice, too. But guilt brings discouragement.

Discouragement is not in anyone's best interest.

CHILD CARE CHOICES

Make sure your child is in safe hands. Look for quality child care. Leaving children in outside care can produce healthy, happy, and well-nurtured children — but it needs to be **quality** child care. Since this means using professional child care services, find out what constitutes such care. (For a detailed guide to finding quality care, including a checklist of what to look for, please refer to *Positive Discipline: The First Three Years* or *Positive Discipline for Preschoolers*, both by Jane Nelsen, Cheryl Erwin, and Roslyn Ann Duffy, Three Rivers Press, Random House, 2007).

If you do not trust your caregivers, find ones you can trust. Your peace of mind will communicate to your child(ren).

CHILD CARE IS EVERYONE'S CONCERN

All children deserve loving environments in which to develop self-esteem, experience emotional well-being, and learn to form healthy connections with others. There is no magic that guarantees such environments exist only at home, with mom, or other relatives. Providing such environments in child care settings or wherever a child spends time away from home is the responsibility of all.

The welfare of any community's children
will affect what the community is and will become
as all of its children grow to adulthood.

Giving birth might result in belly buttons — but childrearing need not result in guilt buttons, no matter where little Ezra sips his daily apple juice.

ALERT: *Please do not sit your child in front of the television for large chunks of the day — whether you are at home with him all the time or only on weekends and evenings. Children need interactive relationships, attention, and ACTIVE play — no matter where their care takes place. Read more about* **Screen Time** *in the chapter on Family Issues.*

Love, Longing, L'inserimento: Waving Good-Bye

Situation

"Mommy, don't go! Please don't go. I want to be with you."

"I don't want to go to school! I hate school!"

"Don't leave me, Daddy. I need a-noth-er h-u-u-g-g. . . . (Hiccup. Sob.)"

Solution: Not So Sweet

How does a parent ever get out the door with pleas like these echoing in her head? Shakespeare might refer to parting as **sweet sorrow**, but few parents find saying good-bye to a tearful child **sweet**. Parting is sad and hard.

LOVE, LONGING, AND L'INSERIMENTO

Waving good-bye is one aspect of a larger process, the three parts of which are: **love**, **longing**, and **l'inserimento**. **Love** refers to **attachment**, that unique connection between a child and his parents. **Longing** is about **separation** — in this case, the pain felt by a parent and child who must be parted. **L'inserimento** is an Italian word, a rough English translation of which is: **insertion, as a key being inserted into a lock**. Another variation in meaning is of being **integrated**. Both of these meanings contribute to a larger emotional concept, that of being **connected through relationships**, referring to the caregiving environment and the people in it.

FINDING THE KEY

Most of the thinking about a child's transition into a new program revolves around **separation**, but **separation** represents only one third (the **longing** part) of the equation. All that takes place before that moment of **separation** has been the development of a child's **attachment** (love) to his family members. What supports successful separation on that first day and beyond, are the new sets of **relationships** that connect the child and his family to a program (**l'inserimento**).

The other side of any good-bye is hello.

EMOTIONAL DEVELOPMENT

Throughout the first years of a child's life she is establishing her emotional framework. **Trust** and **autonomy** are vital to this. **Trust** is learned when a small baby has her needs met. She is fed, changed, held, and comforted.

Autonomy begins in the second year of life when "me do it" becomes her goal. Both of these emotional states are affected when a child is left in the care of others. Both the child and parent need to **trust** the caregivers, while the child needs to experience **separation** in a manner that fosters **autonomy** without feeling like abandonment. **L'inserimento** does that.

DUAL CONNECTION

A child placed in the care of people with whom he has no previous relationship, won't feel that special sense of **l'inserimento** without something developing it. Parents and children need to feel they 'fit in' and can connect to the new program. Those connections are not only with individuals, but also with the program as a whole and the social context of the group setting.

Throughout the steps that have led to a family's enrollment, parents and children have begun to make these connections. A center's philosophy, its physical layout, and the expectations the new family has of the program and the program has of the child and her parent(s) are communicated. These early orientation steps begin the **l'inserimento** process.

ATTACHMENT AND FAMILIARITY

A child's early *attachments* are visible through familiar objects. **Blankies, teddy bears,** or **pacifiers** are typical examples. These represent **the familiar** — and can provide comfort when parents are not present to do so. Such precious items need to be labeled, and ideally are duplicates: one for home and one for school. A private place 'of her very own' (a cubby or any labeled container) where such items can be kept, will provide a tangible connection between home and school.

EARLY CONNECTIONS

People in relationships share time, show interest in, and respect one another.

How can a center build relationships with new parents and children? Some programs do home visits before a child begins attendance (sharing time).

Providing a child with an *Introductory Letter* from the center (see page 96), to be read at home, creates an immediate interaction. Others versions might include a welcome letter or card for the child and his parent(s), or separate ones for each. Photographs of a child's future teacher, a brochure with pictures of the center, or directions to web sites with these images can help, too.

A wonderful book, *The Kissing Hand* by Audrey Penn (Washington, DC: Child & Family Press, 1993), uses kisses planted on one another's palms as a way for a parent and child to stay connected. By pressing one's palm to a cheek, each can feel the other's love — even when they are apart. This is an excellent book to prepare you and your child for the upcoming child care or preschool separations.

PARENT-CHILD VISITS

In Italy, where **l'inserimento** outweighs other priorities, a parent often attends a program with her child for the first weeks. Over that time, the parent takes less and less of an active part as the child integrates (**l'inserimento**) into the program. As the NAEYC publication, *Separation*, edited by Kathe Jarvis characterizes it: *'be boring.'*

WELCOME LETTER

by Roslyn Ann Duffy

Everyone at _____ is feeling excited!
Why do you suppose we are so excited?
We are waiting to meet _____.
That's right — YOU!
You will be coming here very soon and we are waiting for you to get here!
We have a special container ready, with your name on it —
a place for you to put your things.
When you are here with us, we can read stories together.
Perhaps you could bring your favorite story
_____, for us to read, too.
We have lots of yummy things to eat here.
Some of the things you like to eat are

_____.

Your (teachers' names are) (teacher's name is)

_____.

(They are) (She or He is) happy you will be coming here.
You like playing with _____.
We have lots of fun things to play with here, too.
We can sing together. Maybe we can sing

_____,

a song we hear you like.
It won't be too much longer before you will be here.
We are excited to welcome you to

_____.

We'll be waiting for you.

See you soon!

In America, typical orientations include a parent and child visiting **before** the first day of attendance, preferably for an hour or more. All such early connections ease the transitions ahead.

SEPARATION *AND* CONNECTION

Courage is the power to let go of the familiar.
Mary Bryant

Leaving a child in child care is about separation and feelings of sadness. We all **long** for closeness with our loved ones. That **longing**, no matter how much time is spent in relationship building, means that good-byes are still hard.

Leaving one's child in the care of another takes great courage. Children everywhere cry and so do their parents, underscoring the importance of those new hellos.

TIME TO LEAVE

When it is time to leave, tell your child before you go. Give hugs and reassure him that "Mommy will be back" that afternoon or evening. Let a teacher know you are leaving so she can stay with your child while he waves his good-byes.

Support through transition times is vital.

THE WAVING WINDOW

A **waving window** eases the good-bye process. A **waving window** is a place from which a child can see and wave to his parent(s) and mom or dad can wave back. Sometimes parents will use sign language to say "I love you" or give a special wink or signal to send a final message of comfort and care.

A caregiver accompanies each child to the **waving window**, to comfort and hold him.

ROUTINES REASSURE

Routines reassure. Keeping things the same, day after day, helps a child to develop **trust**. Make leave-taking routines predictable.

If daily things stay the same — then the bigger ones,
such as mom or dad's return, can be counted upon to do so, too.

CALL BACK

Parents need reassurance, as well. If a child is in tears, call back an hour or so after leaving. Whether your child has calmed down or not, hearing that he is being tended to will help you breathe easier.

If all of these things are done, everyone should begin to relax and adjust within two or three weeks. Tears will stop or last only a minute or two before a child will be ready to move ahead and enjoy her day.

DELAY

Sometimes this pattern gets reversed. At first everything is new and exciting and, "Oh joy, let me at it"; but sometime around weeks three through six, there is a shift. · A child no longer wants to come to school or she begins crying when mom or dad leaves. The novelty has disappeared. She wants to go back home.

Child care is no longer a great adventure. Her tears are saying, "Stop! I want things to be like they used to be." Sadness replaces enthusiasm.

As before, support, comfort, and reassurance will get parents and children through this tough time. Work on strengthening relationships. Play dates with new classmates, listening to music played at the child care, or singing a center's songs at home can help. Each of these will better connect a child's **home life** to his **school life**.

The bottom-line is that separating is hard and sad —
even if that sadness gets delayed.

CLOSE THE LOOP

Reuniting at day's end closes the **love, longing,** and **l'inserimento** loop.

"See, here I am. I came back for you, just as I said I would."

This is an important part of helping a child to develop **trust**. He needs help to recognize the connection that: *Mommy goes away. She comes back.*

For very young children, the ability to make this connection doesn't exist. The reappearance of someone or something relates to **object permanence**, the understanding that the missing person or object can still exist, even when out of sight. Young children lack this intellectual skill.

OBJECT PERMANENCE

Remember a child covering her face to play 'hide and seek'. If she couldn't see you — you couldn't see her. Such thinking lies at the heart of **object permanence**. Children really cannot understand that someone they cannot see can still see them or will come back to them, because their brains are not yet wired to make sense of this concept.

Even though a child may not have the ability to understand **object permanence**, repetition and pointing out that mom or dad keep returning will strengthen its development.

PROBLEMS

If sadness, anger, or other problems continue past the first few weeks of attendance, something else may be going on. Divorce, illness, or a recent move may make a child too emotionally raw and needy to adjust to additional changes. Schedule a conference to share and explore what else may be going on or has gone on. Being aware of a child's extra neediness during a difficult time makes all the difference.

Though saying good-bye is hard,
behind each good-bye is a doorway that opens to
wonderful new hellos!

#5b
Mealtime Mischief

Meals with little ones
can give a whole new meaning
*to **messy**.*

Meals at Home
a.k.a. Lake Milk

Situation: Spilt Milk and Other Laments

Welcome to mealtime at Nancy's house, and the table she calls Lake Milk.
Ever since her sons, ages two and four, were born, this nickname fits their dining
table to perfection. Each meal includes some form of seeping liquid, which makes
its rapid progress from table to clothes to floor. The daily spills turn every meal
into an ordeal.

Survival instincts warned Nancy to quit serving grape juice months ago. But as
milk splatters over her son's last clean t-shirt, she wants to add her tears to the
already soggy table.

Solution

No one ever said parenting wasn't messy. If your idea of breakfast involves sipping
aromatic coffee, nibbling at warm, fragrant cinnamon rolls, and contemplating the
sun rising over the horizon, Lake Milk is a pretty grim alternative. Even if your
mealtime expectations are more modest, a sloshing table can make anyone
queasy. Let's get practical and deal with the **M.E.S.S.**

THE M.E.S.S.

M.E.S.S. is an excellent acronym for eliminating Lake Milk from the family table.

> **M**istakes happen
> **E**nvironments can be changed
> **S**kills require training
> **S**low down

• *Mistakes Happen*

Even as an adult I tremble at the thought of wearing white clothing. I know that on me, it won't stay pristine for long. We all spill things at times. That is a fact. Another fact is that young children are going to spill — often.

Those tiny hands can barely wrap around a glass. It is a two-fisted achievement to hoist the glass up at all. Imagine trying to drink out of a glass the size of a gallon pickle jar.

There are other physical considerations. Watch young children move. Do they move in a straight line from Point A to Point B? Seldom. They waiver. They wobble. They dawdle. Now imagine moving a large milk-filled container from the table, Point A, to one's mouth, Point B. The fascination of watching little brother stuff an entire muffin into his mouth in one bite creates a detour, quickly leading to a puddle instead of a satisfying swallow of milk.

Expect mistakes. Treat them (mistakes and children) with compassion. Mistakes happen to all of us. Use the rest of the **M.E.S.S** equation to reduce the frequency with which your table will resemble Lake Milk.

• *Environments Can be Changed*

How big is the glass? Can your child reach the table from a sitting position? Is the glass too full? Should the clean t-shirt go on after eating, instead of before?

Look at the overall situation and make changes. Prop a pillow or a fat telephone book under a small child to make the table and its contents accessible. Imagine trying to eat with **your** chin resting on the table. Get cups with spouted caps or lids with straws attached. Some cups won't spill even when knocked over. Make sure glassware is small enough for small hands. Short four-ounce glasses present much less challenge than tall eight-ounce tumblers.

Don't fill glasses to the brim. My own children finally pointed out, when they were in early adolescence, that they felt able to handle a full glass of beverage. (Old habits die hard. I still catch my spouse portioning out a half glass of water when serving me.)

Keep pajama tops on until after the meal. Since you may need to switch into the clean t-shirt anyway, having to remove a milk doused pajama top will not seem like an extra step. Your child will leave the house in a nice clean shirt and you won't be crying over spilt milk, so to speak.

• *Skills are Learned*
There are more skill-building possibilities at mealtime than you may recognize.

Primary skill: .... Managing liquids without spilling
Secondary skills: .... Pouring; mopping up
Physical abilities: .... Eye-hand coordination; muscle coordination

Children love to sop up spills. Teach them how.

BE PREPARED
Making a puddle disappear with a sponge constitutes true magic for a two year old. Demonstrate how to use a sponge before the next mealtime flood. Cut large sponges into pieces that will fit small fingers. Allow children to practice making and removing puddles from the countertop using sponges. Keep a sponge nearby, in a place low enough for a child to reach it without help. Better yet, place a small tray with a sponge on the dining room table, (your choice — **optimism** versus **reality**).

Buy a mop and saw off the handle to make it the right height. Place it nearby, at child level. Next time there is a spill, excellent tools with which to manage the situation are ready and available. Isn't the thought of eager, sturdy, and competent young helpers appealing?

Finally, teach children how to pour. Use a variety of liquids: water, orange juice, and, of course, milk. Introduce different types of unbreakable containers to practice pouring in the bathtub; provide plastic cups and funnels in the sandbox; purchase small watering cans with spouts for watering the household ivy. Have tea parties with tiny, water-filled teapots.

Fill a measuring cup with juice, milk, or another beverage making the container size manageable. Demonstrate the art of pouring. Provide practice: over the sink, on a tray, or at a towel-covered table. Place a similar container in the refrigerator. Children can pour milk on morning cereal, cups of juice for snacks, and even serve morning juice to their appreciative parents.

SLOW DOWN

Haste makes mess.

Plan more time for meals. Mopping up spills, changing shirts and pants, and allowing children to serve themselves takes time. It takes time to avoid spills and it takes time to clean them up. Be prepared to do both.

ENJOY

Focus on mealtime connecting instead of mealtime messes. Talk over the day instead of warning everyone to "Be careful"; "Watch that you don't spill that"; or saying, "That is going to spill" until everyone would love to pour any beverage onto you know whose head.

Watch your children learn to manage the many skills, implements, and liquids coming their way each day. Your mealtimes won't resemble television commercials for exotic coffees, but they will become more pleasant family times. Someday soon you might all lift your glasses in a mealtime toast, maybe even using real grape juice.

FINAL TIP:

If all else fails, consider getting a dog —
one that laps up juice, milk, and gravy
with equal gusto.

MEALTIME

M.E.S.S.

Mistakes happen
Environments can be changed
Skills take practice
Slow down, digest more

Dare to Dine Out

Situation: Eating in Public

Last week my sister-in-law took our family to brunch at an elegant restaurant. Our family consists of my husband, our three-year-old daughter, ten-month-old baby girl, and me. Disaster does not begin to describe the meal.

Our three year old spent her time hiding under the tablecloth and tickling people's feet, or darting off between tables, once nearly tripping a passing waiter. The waiter was balancing a tray full of drinks (all of which were guaranteed to stain, I'm sure).

I won't even mention what the baby did, but it involved me spending most of the meal in the ladies' room (one not equipped for babies), but at least we had it to ourselves. After one whiff, all the other occupants fled.

I figure we won't be eating out for at least the next 20 years.

Solution

Young children, lots of adult observers, and few child-friendly amenities are guaranteed to equal disaster. One of the hardest things for most of us to handle is figuring out how to discipline a child in public. We want to be regarded by the rest of the world as rational, civilized people. Dealing with a wily youngster amidst crystal glassware or changing a baby on a marble powder room countertop does not bring out the best of these traits.

We all have many **shoulds** reverberating in our heads. They sound like this:

"You should be a better parent."
"You should be able to control the behavior of a three year old." (Ha!)
"You shouldn't let your child get away with such behavior."

Let's just tell the **should** tapes to pipe down for a moment. Instead of the **shoulds**, let's proceed to the three Ps.

Prevent. Prepare. Practice.

PREVENT

The best discipline is often prevention. Take a good look at your dining partners. Does your three year old have a fondness for mushroom canapés? Is she content to sit at a table for an hour or more? Is she adept with forks, glassware, and lace-edged napkins? Probably not.

Does your ten month old usually require a bath after mealtime? Is her bowel timed to erupt right after eating? Do you really want to perform these cleaning functions in a velvet-lined powder room in front of a roomful of silk-clad women busily freshening their lipstick? Do they want you to?

After taking inventory of the 'raw material' represented by your proposed eating companions, consider the type of dining experience best matching their abilities and overall needs. Chances are, the elegant hotel brunch will not top the list.

NEEDS

What are the needs or reason for this meal? If dining at the town's new, fancy hotel is a must, get a sitter. If being together as a family is the priority, go somewhere else. If speed is the need, go to a cafeteria. There will be plenty of choices and no waiting. If your child cannot handle the decorum needed for **any** restaurant, order take-out food and slurp it up at home.

Meet the needs — change the details.

PREPARE

After evaluating needs and abilities, share expectations with the children. Talk over the plans. Of course the baby can't share in this discussion, but from two-and-a-half years on, young children can be involved in preparations for outings.

Start by asking your child what sort of things people do in a restaurant. Answers to suggest if your child does not include them are: **sit in chairs**; **use forks and spoons for eating**; and **wipe hands with napkins**. (This does not imply that home meals are eaten at a trough; it just gives children an opportunity to visualize the proposed outing.)

Ask your child what behavior is **not acceptable** in a restaurant. Cover such topics as: **no running inside**; **salt and pepper stay in their shakers**; **only quiet voices are used inside**; and **we sit in our seats** — we do not climb over (or under) them.

I am sure you can think of additional things to add to both of these lists, just be sure to give your child every opportunity to name them himself, rather than turn this into a lecture of dos and don'ts. The more your child is involved in the conversation, the better he will visualize and act upon the plans.

PRACTICE

Practice includes two parts — yours and theirs. The first part is to give children time to practice dining skills in simple and undemanding settings. As skills develop, the difficulty level increases. This may mean starting at fast food places with an occasional foray into the local family diner, followed by a grand celebration at some place that uses actual tablecloths (albeit plastic-coated ones). You probably won't reach the level of hotel brunch for quite awhile (years even).

The second part of practice is to **practice what you preach**. This is the hard part. You have practiced prevention by scaling your expectations to your child's needs and abilities. You prepared thoroughly and involved your child in planning. So when sitting at Dolly's Delightful Diner, and little Anna hurtles across the room and starts making faces at the octogenarians two booths away, you act. This is **your** practice time.

Back there in the planning session, one of the things that needed to be included was a clear understanding of what you (the adult) intended to do if certain behaviors occurred in the restaurant. It might sound like this: "If you do not stay seated at the table, we'll go to the car and wait there until you are ready to go back in and try again." Many parents actually say something along these lines, but when the situation occurs, nothing happens. Instead they might say:

"Remember what I said about staying in your seat?"
"You better get back in your seat before I count to three . . . One . . . Two . . . Two-and-a-half . . . Two-and-three-quarters . . . "
"If you don't get back in your seat we're going to have to go out to the car . . . "

Stop talking. You told your child what you planned to do. He remembers. Now do it. Ask if he wants to hold your hand and walk or have you carry him to the car. YOU ARE NOT ANGRY when you do this. You are CALM. You are KIND. You are both HEADED TO THE CAR.

Sit in the car a few moments; when he stops screaming, ask, "Are you ready to try again?" I realize that by now your french fries have congealed on your plates, but once your child trusts that you will do what you say you will do, he won't need to keep testing it out.

If the second try at sitting in the restaurant fizzles, it is time to ask that your meal be boxed for take-out as you and your child wait in the car for the rest of the family to finish and join you. Though this process sounds grim, children learn quickly. Think about that. What are they learning if you don't do what you say you will do?

IMPORTANT CAUTION:

Beware of what you say!

BON APPETIT!

Prevent, **Prepare**, and **Practice** can make dining out digestible — for everyone. Your children will be delightful dining companions, even if the restaurants are less than four star. Enjoy!

DO YOUR BEST:

If that fancy restaurant is inescapable, adapt these plans and do your best.

• Bring along dry cereal or raisins to keep little fingers busy and make the wait less stressful.

• Provide paper and crayons for older children.

• Always — ASK FOR EXTRA NAPKINS!!

Mealtime Mischief

Situation: Making Mealtime More Digestible for All

Here are three mealtime mischief-making scenarios:

#1: I spend the entire meal saying, "Alexander, you need to eat." The rest of the family finishes while I am still at the table coaxing him.

#2: Our daughter, Breanne, who just turned three, monopolizes our evening dinners: talking the whole time; interrupting others; or getting up and running around, which means chasing her down to bring her back to her place.

*#3: Our son, Jose is four. He says, "I hate this," as soon as he comes to the table. **This** could be anything. He says he hates **it** before he even sees what **it** is. Most nights I end up giving him a bowl of cereal. Some nights I have to make a special trip to the store because we have run out of cereal, but he won't eat anything else.*

Solution: Indigestion or Survival?

Does your mealtime motto seem to be: 'Indigestion for all'?

Has the butting of heads supplanted the breaking of bread at your table? Do you spend more time 'chewing out' your children than chewing your food? Are family feasts more frustrating than festive?

What are mealtimes like at your house? What would you like them to be? Have you thought about it?

WHY EAT?

The first question really is: **why do we eat**? What is the purpose of eating in your house? Is it to fill bellies, enjoy food, and spend time together or is it a rushed interruption in an overscheduled day?

A few weeks ago, I insisted a friend get her cup of coffee in a take-out cup because we didn't have time to sit in the café while she drank it. My friend, a native of France, told me that in France, "We don't use take-out cups. Drinking coffee is time to be with friends." We sat. She sipped. We enjoyed a relaxed half-hour together.

- What if your child hungers for attention more than food? Did you take time to enjoy each other today?
- What if your child isn't hungry at mealtime? Is a carrot eaten as a snack less nutritious than those in the evening soup?
- What if your child eats only junk food? Who does your grocery shopping?

THANKFULNESS

In much of the world food is scarce and survival a struggle. In cultures where food is abundant, it is easy to forget its value. Mealtimes are meant to be happy occasions: times to connect with one another; share the day's news; and break bread with those we love.

Around the world people come together to eat and give thanks. Beginning meals with rituals: a time of prayer; moments of silence; or a linking of hands establishes an atmosphere that honors this time together.

THINK ABOUT IT.

What happens at your dinner table? Alexander's dad listened to himself and discovered how often he repeated his, "You need to eat your food now," warnings as Alexander ignored them. Why did he keep saying it? When he asked himself that question, he had no answer.

Why did Alexander ignore him? Why not? He knew dad would keep saying the same thing, do nothing, and continue to give him his complete attention.

Attention is attention and children will take what they can get.

Alexander, the youngest of four children, had found a way to get his dad to himself. The payoff at the meal's end was even better. The longer he could make his string beans, potatoes, or chicken nuggets last, the longer he 'had him'.

HUSH. HUSH.

For the next week, Alexander's dad decided to limit himself to two warnings (he couldn't bear to say nothing at all). He also decided to leave the table even if Alexander was still eating.

The first time he got up, Alexander tried to get dad (and the attention) back by stirring ketchup into his milk. That got mom to return, but only to say, "Looks like you have finished. Let's clear your plate. You may help me clean up the table."

Clearing the table together was attention, but the kind it is good to encourage. Helping mom gave Alexander a way to contribute and feel noticed.

By the end of the week Alexander was eating most of his dinner — without reminders. If he dallied, dad kept quiet. The rest of the family talked about their day and everyone's digestion improved.

HEAD OF THE TABLE

Breanne's family took a look at their mealtime, too. Breanne kept things hopping at her house and she was in a great position to do so. Why? Because Breanne sat at the head of the table — front and center. The only thing she lacked was a spotlight.

On one side of the table sat mom, across from her sat Breanne's older sister Anika, and tucked into the corner, sat dad. Those table positions said a lot. Dad's seat, wedged between the table and wall made it hard for him to get up. Who chased Breanne and returned her to her place at the table? You guessed it — mom.

Meanwhile, Anika's seat relegated her to the sidelines, physically and metaphorically. Anika's attempts to talk couldn't compete with Breanne's center stage performance.

Breanne's parents decided to redo their seating plan. Dad moved his chair next to mom's and Breanne got dad's old seat by the wall, which had the added advantage of making it harder for her to get in and out. No one sat at the head of the table.

They told Breanne that when she got up they would assume she was finished eating; then she would need to clear her plate and find something quiet to do while the rest of the family finished. They put these changes into effect at the next meal.

Mom and dad also looked for more productive ways to give Breanne attention outside of mealtime. Mom and Breanne would read a story together while dinner cooked; Breanne and Anika would help dad set out the silverware and plates; and they might all take a short walk before or after dinner.

Meals grew calmer. Breanne became part of the family instead of its focal point. Without all the jumping up and down, Anika could tell about her school projects and reconnect with her parents, something they realized they had been missing.

YUCK! WHAT'S THAT?
Instead of starting each meal by getting upset when Jose would say he 'hates' whatever was for dinner, mom suggested beginning meals by naming one thing

each of them felt happy about that day. She invited Jose to go first, which gave him instant positive attention.

Mom also invited Jose to help her with planning menus and cooking, providing both a new perspective and special time together. He would wash the potatoes for baking, stir the muffin batter, and tear lettuce leaves for the evening's salad. Jose liked hearing comments on things he had helped prepare. This new attention resulted in less interest in the old kind he had gotten by complaining.

Though some complaints still happen, with less attention, they happen less. Now, if Jose says he doesn't like tonight's broiled trout, his mom says, "Let's remember that when we plan next week's menu so you can suggest something you do like if we are having trout."

Last of all, mom thought about the cereal beckoning from the kitchen cupboard. If she didn't buy them, Jose wouldn't be able to eat them. Or if she did buy them, but not replace them until the next week's grocery shopping, then if he ate them all in the first day or two, there wouldn't be any left. If he chose not to eat after they ran out, she would say and do nothing, trusting that he would not starve (for her, the hardest part of all!).

Jose will still make an occasional dinner of cereal, but since they're available less, he is discovering that the rest of the food isn't so 'yucky' and at no point has he been in danger of starvation.

FEEDING THE REAL HUNGER

Hunger makes our bellies rumble, but in our spirits we feel a different hunger. We need attention and time to connect with one another. We need to feed both our bodies and our spirits. Post a new mealtime motto at your house — today.

Calm, cooperation, and bon appetit to all.

Childhood Obesity

Situation: Too Much National Growth

I am having a difficult time getting clothes to fit my five year old. The length of her pants is right, but she cannot zip them up because of her tummy (well, actually she isn't the only one with this problem!). Can a child this young be overweight?

Solution: It Isn't the Clothes

Unfortunately, your daughter's sweet belly is not baby fat. These days we hear more than ever about children's weight — and with good reason. According to the *American Obesity Association,* the percentage of obese children more than doubled (7% to 15.3%) from mid-1970 to 2000, while the adolescent rate tripled (5% to 15.5%). Related to this shift is the appearance of Type II Diabetes, a disease once unheard of in children, but which can lead to everything from heart problems to kidney failure. Estimates are that 2.7 million adolescents are at risk for developing this disease, in addition to the 39,000 who already have it.

It seems that we and our children have become as fat-drenched as the 1.85 billion pounds of chips we eat each year; more sugar-laden than the 20+ teaspoons of sugar our daily taste buds crave; and more loaded with extras than the 23 pounds (about 1/2 pound a week) per person of pizza that we consume annually. But food is simply part of the problem and putting children on diets only piles on emotional poundage. A better approach is to slow weight gain and allow children to grow into added weight, a process that can take months or years — and requires a lifestyle change.

LIFESTYLE CHANGE BACK

Perhaps what we need to look at is not **lifestyle change** but rather a **lifestyle change back**. We haven't always been pudgy people — so what about our lifestyle is different and what can we learn from past lifestyle choices to help us improve upon today's? Thinking back, I came up with three differences that might offer some useful clues.

The rule in our family was that my brothers and I had to come inside "when the streetlights went on."

Where were we? Outside. True, I grew up in Arizona where the weather made year-round outdoor play easier, but my husband spent similar hours outdoors on the lots and streets around his New York City home in Queens. While I played hide-and-seek, practiced hopscotch, and plotted water balloon strategies, he was enjoying stickball, playing tag along city sidewalks, or pitching countless innings of catch, with occasional tosses to the family dog. (According to the *National Research Council,* one-fourth of today's dogs and cats are also obese).

And of course, we all walked and rode bikes. Which brings me to item #2.

We had a lot of personal mobility.

Bicycles gave us access to wide neighborhood territories. We had to get from place to place on our own since most of us were one-car families (at best). When we wanted to play at a friend's house (many of whom lived nearby), we had to get there without parent chauffeurs. Walking (or running), bicycling, and later, public transportation were the means for getting to local grocery stores, swimming pools, or the neighborhood playground. All of which worked up healthy appetites; hence we arrive at item #3.

We ate in — not out.

Eating out was expensive and reserved for special treats, like the occasional Friday night fish and chips at Pete's Drive-In — memories of which still bring back mouthwatering nostalgia. Such times, by their rarity, became memorable.

Even though both of my parents worked, our family ate dinner at home and together (a practice now linked to both higher grades and lower drug and alcohol abuse). Often these meals were prepared in haste, as we all joined in to tear lettuce into pieces, season meat for broiling, or mash the night's potatoes. By now, you may expect me to recall the miles I trudged through slush and snow to get to that one-room schoolhouse on the prairie (we did walk to school, but it only took about ten minutes, less if we made an effort), but even without one-room schoolhouses, life today is different.

BASIC CHANGES

Safety issues or crowded city living make even the idea of children roaming neighborhoods downright unthinkable. Even if it were safe to do so — by the time most parents finish work and children wrap up their sports practices, music or art lessons, and wade through the night's homework, streetlights will have long been burning.

And who has the energy to cook a meal at the end of a 12-hour day? Having said all of that, if we condense my three items down to their essentials, what we have are these:

1. Physical activity and outdoor time
2. Less car time
3. Basic (unprocessed) food

These three items are a close match for similar conclusions reported by the *Journal of the American Medical Association* on trends that may relate to today's childhood obesity: sedentary lifestyle (items #1 and #2); consumption of fast foods (item #3); and portion size, something much easier to control at home (item #3).

Another study in the *Journal of School Health* zeroes in on **screen time**, associating television viewing with decreased activity (item #1) and contributing to both unhealthy food choices (through food advertising) and increased snacking (item #3).

With these in mind, here are a few ways we can begin to **change back** our lifestyles and still remain in the 21st century.

LIFESTYLE CHANGE BACKS: PHYSICAL ACTIVITY

The easiest way to encourage physical activity is to unplug (or limit) use of 'screens' (i.e., televisions, computer, and electronic toys). Watching television more than two hours daily has been linked to obesity. Without 'screen' time, children will find other things to do and eat fewer high-fat snacks. It may not be comforting information for tired parents, but the *National Association for Sport and Physical Education* tells us that toddlers and preschoolers shouldn't stay sedentary (sit still) for more than 60 minutes at a time, unless they are sleeping. Whew!

At least we can encourage their movement (without any of our own) by providing props such as hula-hoops; inflatable balls for bouncing on; and trikes to ride on enclosed decks, in fenced backyards, or down hallways. Of course, children also do what they see and overweight parents increase a child's risk of becoming overweight.

Our lifestyle and theirs go hand in hand. If you must keep the tube on — consider using exercise tapes together or try dancing with tambourines, maracas, or bells as you jump around and make noise. Moving together is fun!

LIFESTYLE 'CHANGE BACKS': CAR TIME

Let's move on — or more to the point — move on our own. It is true that outdoor time is not the option it once was but we can get out of those cars. Among one daughter's favorite memories were the special times we shared when she and I walked together to her child care or school. It was time all to ourselves — with exercise as a side bonus. A group in Seattle, Washington, has begun an organization called *Feet First* to promote what they describe as a 'Walking School

Bus.' They recruit parents and nearby seniors to accompany groups of children to school, opting out of using the school bus. The children arrive alert after a healthy walk; and with up to 25% of morning traffic related to transporting children to schools, a resurgence of walking means healthier air to breathe, perhaps triggering less asthma (another growing childhood problem).

It takes about 20 minutes to walk a slow-paced mile. Can you or your child walk for 20 minutes? Get out a neighborhood map and draw a circle with a one-mile radius from your home. Is there a library, grocery store, or park in that radius? If so, go there, have fun, rest a bit; and then walk another 20 minutes home again. This timeframe is close to the recommended 30-minutes of 'moderate physical activity' described in the *Journal of School Health.*

If 20 minutes is the maximum time available, give your circle a half-mile radius or simply walk for 10 minutes, turn around and come back home. Sometimes the battle to buckle seatbelts takes at least that long. You may be amazed at how close things really are and as your child gains skills, bicycling can increase the distances traveled.

LIFESTYLE CHANGE BACKS: EATING IN

Are you hungry yet? What, where, and who will provide that next meal? A key we discovered (my husband and I both worked full time) was very basic: PLANNING. The following strategies can make all the difference between eating in — and not bulging out (of those clothes).

Plan Weekly Menus

We made up a menu for the coming week, often as part of family meeting discussions, so that all family members got to have their say. If I made the stuffed peppers that several of us liked, I would include applesauce and baked potatoes for those who hated peppers. This was not easy, but it paid off (cooperation is a primary aim of all discipline) and allowed us to use the next tip to our advantage.

Shop Once-A-Week

Make a grocery list based upon the week's menu. We did one main shopping trip each week and when it was time to prepare a meal, all of the ingredients were available. This eliminated last-minute trips to the store when we were at our most tired, hungry, and cranky. The best discipline of all is prevention!

Hire Help *(the permanent/non-human kind)*
No, we did not have a *Cordon Bleu* chef, but we did have some five-star appliances: a crockpot or slow cooker, a bread machine, and a freezer.

Before leaving for work in the morning, we would load the crockpot with veggies and seasonings and the bread machine with flour and yeast and 8 or 10 hours later, enter a house fragrant with the aromas of fresh-baked bread and tomato-ey rich soup. Get out the bowls and dinner was served.

The freezer was our other main kitchen partner. When my husband made a batch of cherry muffins or I rolled up a recipe of enchiladas, we would double or triple the recipes and have one meal that day and another frozen, ready to pop into the microwave as soon as we burst through the door. Dinner was ready almost before we had time to scatter our raincoats around the house. Freezing extras also makes it easier for a single parent and child to enjoy variety as well as prepare full-size recipes and save by buying foods in larger quantities.

Streetlights May Be On — But Pounds Needn't Be
These are not the only solutions to a lifestyle **change back** nor are they always possible, but thinking about ways to tweak your lifestyle to encourage more physical activity; reframe your transportation to exclude cars whenever possible; or find ways to enjoy the fruits and vegetables of your own labors — well, maybe everyone's zipper could be a bit easier to close.
Even Fido might have a few less pounds to hoist the next time he leaps up to greet you beneath that streetlight's fading glow.

PRACTICAL TIP

Eliminate soda pop and there is a good chance you will reduce weight gain, too.

#5c

Bedtime Blues

Day is done, but does sleep seem
like a foggy memory?
Whether dealing with bedtime battles or
midnight wakings, if you peer out at each new day
through weary eyes — here is a bedtime prescription.

Bedtime Prescription

Situation: Bleary-Eyed Parents with Bright-Eyed Midnight Marvels

HELP! I have a two-and-a-half-year-old son who is difficult to get to sleep, and even worse, he insists on sleeping in my bed! How can I get him to fall asleep in his own bed? He is forever getting up.

I've tried lying down with him until he goes to sleep (but so do I). I've tried rocking him to sleep — but he wakes up as soon as I try to lay him down. Then I lose it and start spanking him every time he gets up. We cannot continue on like this. I am VERY DESPERATE!

Solution

Bedtime parenting takes perspective, lots of patience, and saint-like persistence. The perspective is that of figuring out what we want and why — based on the BIG picture of the life skills we want our children to have. The patience and persistence are how we achieve the desired goal.

That time of day when parents feel weary, wiped out, and ready to crawl between their own waiting sheets — when all we want to do is go to sleep and have our child(ren) do the same, presents a challenge. We want this child in his own bed, right? Or do we?

SOUL SEARCHING

What is the BIG picture? What is it you want? If you feel at all ambiguous about *whether* you want your child to sleep alone, *whether* you feel you need to lie with him, or *whether* you feel he will be safe away from your side — he will sense your uncertainty.

What is it you really want? Do you feel guilty? Why? What is best for you and your child? There are no **right** or **wrong** answers, only the answers that are **right** for your situation.

Once you are clear about what you want, can resolve your own feelings of guilt, and determine what will work best for everyone's needs, your son will sense that, too.

A PLAN

If the mom in the original question decides she really wants her son in his own bed, then she needs to explain that to him **during the day**. She can tell him how much she loves him and that she realizes she sleeps better when he is not in her bed. She can express confidence that he will rest best in his own bed.

Now comes the hard part.

GET READY TO FOLLOW THROUGH

Carrying out a new bedtime plan is going to take patience and persistence — both aspects of **following through** on what we say we will do. Someone who is exhausted before dinner even begins will be a candidate for mayhem by bedtime. Don't let that someone be YOU!

Take care of yourself. Take a bath or shower if that helps you unwind. A single parent or one home alone, might bring her child into the shower or bath with her. If you are uncomfortable with this and your child is too young to leave unattended while you are in the bath, trade babysitting with a neighbor for an hour every afternoon so you have time to refresh your frazzled spirit. Single parents **must** find a support network. Support is **not** a luxury, but a necessity. Get it. Everyone will benefit.

SLOW DOWN. RECONNECT.

Slow down. Relax with a cup of tea after dinner (ignore the dishes — look the other way). Your child might enjoy sipping his own cup of herbal tea or warm milk along with you. Get small cups to create a **special teatime** atmosphere. Roll your head, circle your shoulders, and let your muscles relax — breathe.

Couples, as well as children and parents, need to spend a few moments reconnecting with one another, and talking over the day. (Many of you are choking on laughter at this point. "Yeah, right. Time to talk to each other — are you kidding?") Again — NOT optional! Sip hot soup out of mugs while sitting on the bathroom floor as little Janie splashes in her evening bath. Soup sipped in harmony beats chewing steak with clenched teeth any day. When we believe something is important (i.e., our own needs), we find time.

But some parental needs do need to move to the back burner. The parent determined to sink into a favorite chair in front of the television or read the newspaper is almost guaranteed to find himself (or herself) issuing threats, battling with a mate, or listening to a wailing child before the last cock crows.

YOUR CHILD'S NEEDS

Is your child ready to sleep? Has she had a chance to reconnect with you? Make sure she is tired. Go for a walk after dinner, maybe take an evening swim class together or go to a park for some running and exercise on the climbers. All of these provide time to reconnect as well as to burn off excess energy. If your child takes a long afternoon nap, he may not be quite ready to fall asleep by 8:00 p.m. Active play will help him expend energy and feel more ready to sleep.

Perhaps his bedtime resistance is his way of saying he wants more time with you. These activities also meet his needs for your time and attention and provide together time for both of you.

BEDTIME ROUTINES

Routines diminish resistance. Routines turn everyday events into habits — and no one really thinks about habitual behaviors. Keep bedtime routines simple — with no more than five steps.

Brush teeth. Put on pajamas. Read. Hug. Tuck into bed.

A bedtime routine works wonders. Children under three enjoy helping decorate a bedtime list of activities. With an older or more verbal child, ask for suggestions; listen to his ideas and then work together to plan a nightly bedtime routine.

PERSISTENCE

You calmed yourself, you spent an hour at the park with your child, and you have followed the established routine, including lots of nice cuddling. Little Jason is all tucked in and you are channel surfing for your favorite program.

Pitter, patter, flap, flop.

The sound of plastic pajama feet is unmistakable, as your child makes a beeline to your side. Now what?

He is checking to see if you really meant what you said. What did you say? You said, "If you get up — I will walk you back to your bed." So, walk — don't talk.

If he resists say, "Do you want to walk, hold my hand, or be carried?" Stay calm. Get him back into bed. Even if you must repeat this trip a few (or many) times, try to stay calm, consistent, and caring. This is a pretty big order, especially at night when relaxed or not, you are simply tired.

Your persistence needs to match his resistance.

Perhaps you headed straight to your own bed. If he comes into your room, walk or carry him back to his bed. Offer him a chance to return on his own. Remember to breathe.

What if he cries? Face it – **if** is very unlikely. **When** is the probable reality. Again, decide on what you will do. Some parents find that it only takes a night or two of crying (with luck, your child is doing the crying and not you) before everyone settles into the new bedtime routine.

Other parents choose to return to a crying child and offer a soothing word or comfort him with an additional hug and tuck-in. Neither approach will make listening to his cries easy, but your attitude (remember the soul searching) will make it tolerable.

If you see learning to fall asleep on his own or in his own bed as a valuable life skill, or the need for both of you to get a sound sleep as a top priority — then the short-term discomfort will be manageable (for all).

Whichever approach is used, whether you believe your child should remain in the 'family bed' or not, bedtime can proceed with minimal fuss if the underlying attitude of the adult is clear. When we know what we want and believe it is the best choice, we succeed in doing what it takes to achieve the results we want.

BEDTIME PRESCRIPTION
Decide what you want, what you and your child need, and what you are willing to do to achieve it. Prepare your child for bedtime with active play; follow a consistent bedtime routine; give him your focused attention.

Take care of yourself; postpone some of your own activities; get needed support from a partner or other source. When tuck-in time comes around, parent(s) will feel calm, child(ren) will be tired, and expectations will be clear. That's a great prescription for a sound night's sleep — for everyone.

Remember:
*Preparing a suitable environment for sleep
is something the adult can do;
actually falling asleep — only the child can do.*

Whose Bed is This?

Situation: Whose Bed is This?

We are not sleeping well at all. Every night, in the middle of the night, our three year old shows up and climbs into bed with us. She gets between my husband and me, flops around; and we each end up clinging to the sides of the bed as she sprawls in the middle.

If I take her back to her room she starts fussing. Her dad is threatening to sleep in the guest room so he can get a decent sleep. I am exhausted. Either way, I end up being awake half the night. Help!

Solution

FIRST — EXAMINE YOUR HEART

The first and biggest step for each of you is to acknowledge your own feelings about having your daughter in bed with you. This is a hot button issue that can tap into one's deepest values and beliefs. Whatever the reasons, the reality is that if either parent is feeling guilty, ambiguous, or unsure about whether a child should sleep in her own bed or not, whatever those feelings are will outweigh any actions attempted.

In other words, if you feel guilty or really like having your daughter in bed with you — then trying to get her to sleep in her own bed or room won't work. Why? She will sense those feelings and respond to them — rather than to your words or actions.

If, on the other hand, you feel that learning to sleep in her own room through the night is an important life skill — then her fussing, and your mutual discomfort with making this change, will be manageable. She will get the message that you mean what you say, as well as that she is loved and cared for.

SECOND — COMMIT TO A PLAN

After accepting how you really feel, then make a plan that you can commit to. If you feel your child is too young to (or shouldn't) sleep alone, or you simply want to extend this special cuddly time together, then decide what you are willing to do to accommodate her late night arrivals.

As long as both partners agree that sharing the family bed is desirable — then suitable accommodations can be found. One parent choosing to sleep in a different room needn't be seen as a threat, but as a reasonable choice. It may also mean finding time for an afternoon nap to get some needed rest.

Such a decision, however, may not be one to which both partners agree. For couples, a child in bed brings up the issue of their sex life (or maybe its absence). These are difficult and often contentious choices for couples to make, but if the discussion begins with one's deepest feelings, then the challenges will be surmountable.

If you decide that the ideas mentioned above are not acceptable and still feel conflicted about sending your daughter from your bed, then you need to consider other solutions such as: getting a bigger bed; setting out a small bed or sleeping bag beside yours; or finding an alternate way to get your own needed rest. Honoring one's feelings is the starting point for whatever modifications are chosen — or not.

NOT 'OUR' BED

If you have resolved your feelings of guilt and place a high value on helping your child learn to stay in her own bed, then deciding on a timetable and plan of action are the next steps. This might mean sitting down with your daughter and talking about how tired you are and that you want everyone to get a better night's sleep.

Discuss how you will walk (or carry) her back to her room and tuck her into her own bed, rather than have her spend the rest of the night in yours. Do this in a caring way as you reassure her that you love her and know she will sleep better in her own bed.

DO IT
One mom recalls walking her daughter back to bed and tucking her in 17 times (she counted). That was a long night for both of them, but don't you have to admire this child's persistence (a trait she and her mom seem to share!)?

Another father remembers the 45-minute tantrum his son pitched the first night they tried their new plan (an outburst dad timed as he lay rigid in his bed, counting the seconds). The next night the crying lasted 30 minutes and by the third night it was over in 10 minutes. After that it was over for good. Bedtime became peaceful for both of them.

Tip: Timing is everything.
Put a new plan into action on a weekend or vacation time,
when everyone can sleep in.

Enduring a few nights of such struggles is not for the feint of heart. That is why the initial step of really examining your own feelings is crucial.

Most of us resist change of any kind. Change sets off alarm bells inside our brains, triggering a **change back** response. The **change back** message is: "Do it the old/familiar way". This message is the same even when the **old/familiar way** wasn't working.

One more example helps provide perspective.

Resistance does end.

In this third family, their three-year-old girl had the habit of waking up in the middle of the night, much like our family in the original scene. Her parents decided it was time for her to stay in her own bed and told her of this expectation. The first night mom walked her back to her own bed. The next night this child got creative. She didn't come into her parents' bed, but instead, dragged her blankie and pillow down the hall and camped in their doorway. Her parents made no comment as they stepped over her the next the morning. Longtime parents (she was not their first born), they actually marveled at how resourceful she was and thought her ingenuity was awesome. It only took a few nights before their daughter decided to stay in her own bed all night.

SAY IT — DO IT

The crucial step is to **do** whatever you **say** (or decide) you will do. Get to the store and find that bigger bed or set up the guest room to make a comfortable sleeping space, then relax and cuddle up with your little one.

If you want your bed back, be prepared to walk/carry your child to her bed however many times (and nights) it takes. Gird yourself to listen to her outrage. Commit to staying calm, kind, and firm throughout this transition.

Whatever you decide — once you do it — everyone should start enjoying more restful nights, as well as peace of mind.

Sweet dreams.
Sleep tight and —
Good night.

#6

Sibling Fights

At last we reach problem #6: Sibling Fights.
The good news is that if you only have one child,
you can skip this chapter since the only people
who list this problem have more than one child.
But with more than one child —
there are going to be, well, issues!
*Think **relationships and skills** instead of*
***whodunit** and you'll be on the right track.*

"She Hit Me First!"

Situation: What To Do When Siblings Fight

"It is not!" "Is so," echoed down the hallway as a neighbor walked into Sunieh's kitchen. *"What's going on?"* she asked.

"The usual. I think they're fighting over whose turn it is to pick a television program. I can't decide if I should unplug the set or buy earplugs. They've been at it all afternoon and I'm worn out!"

Does this sound familiar? Could it be your house? If you have more than one child or were raised with brothers and/or sisters, you know about sibling fighting.

Solution: Choose Me

Why do brothers and sisters fight? A basic reason is that each wants exclusive rights to mom or dad's love, time, and attention. They also fight because they live together and it takes skills to live with others. Children lack skills and skills take time and effort to learn.

Since much of sibling fighting begins with **perspective**, let's start there.

Perspective is everything.

Perspective changes everything and every perspective is different.

On a trip to California our family stayed at my brother's home. One of our children slept on the top bunk in the blue-painted bedroom; the other on the sofa in the adjacent family room. From the perspective of the child on the bunk: "My brother got to sleep on the sofa and mom made **his** bed for him every night."

From the perspective of the sofa dweller: "My sister got the **nice** bed while I was stuck on the sofa."

Same situation — different perspectives.

WHODUNIT?

Perspective aside, we adults are often tempted to try sorting out children's fights, **who** did **what** to **whom,** as if life were a mystery novel. We might have seen Bobby grab Sally's book and felt justified in sending Bobby to his room. What we might not have seen, five minutes earlier, was Sally hiding Bobby's baseball cards under the table. Either way — **equal** treatment is better than attempting to be judge and jury.

"Both of you go to your rooms. You may come out when you can play without fighting." This response focuses not on **whodunit**, but on the need for the fighting to end. Being yelled at or singled out for punishment, though negative, is still attention and any attention risks sending an unspoken message.

Once your back is turned to bawl out Anna, little Katie's tears transform into a gloating smile, until you turn again, when Katie's tears magically reappear. Both Anna and Katie understand that smile. It says, "Ha-ha! Mommy loves me best." Children decode **attention** with this unspoken message, even if the attention is negative.

LAUGH AND HUG

Defusing a situation with humor and love can work miracles.

Another day I entered our living room to find two of my daughters suspended upside down, heads dangling off the sofa while conducting a tug-of-war over a soccer sock, each shouting, "It's mine."

"Please, don't move. I have to get a picture of this," I said, reaching for my camera. Quicker than my flash, the battle was over. They laughed, rolled off the sofa and said, "Mom, you're weird."

The soccer sock was forgotten and we shared a big hug.

EVALUATE

In the absence of blood, broken bones, or demolished tables — it is best to stay out of children's squabbles. Imagine you are on a movie set. The director yells "Action!" The family rumpus roars onstage. Children chase one another; roll around on the floor; arms, legs, and heads tangling together. Your first urge is to leap out of your chair, separate bodies, and issue threats. Resist this urge.

Take a deep breath and **evaluate**. Remember watching puppies play? They bat at each other, nip, yelp, and maybe practice a few snarls. Is this what you are seeing in front of you? Are your children at all like puppies in this moment? Is their play wild but not deadly? If so, let the cameras keep rolling. Find something else to do if you can't bear to stay and watch.

ACT

Act instead of react.

If, upon evaluation, you believe that one, both, or all children will be truly harmed — **stop the action**. Separate the combatants. Perform emergency first aid, letting the non-injured help the wounded. This is called damage control. Clear the set and take a break. "It looks like you are very upset. We all need some time to cool off."

Send children to separate rooms, a common room, or the same bench — **none** being allowed to get up until **all** are willing to talk — without fighting.

GUIDE

Once calm is restored, call the cast back onto the set for a consultation. Good directors guide their performers through the problem-solving process. Listen. Give each child a turn to tell his story. Let's say Mary threw a shoe at her brother Sam.

Mary's version is, "He took my teddy bear and was going to throw it in the toilet." (Be sure Sam does not interrupt until Mary is finished. His turn is coming.)

Then Sam says, "I was only teasing. And look at the mark her shoe made." At this point Sam holds up Exhibit A, a red line on his arm.

Mary rebuts with her defense, "It was an accident!"

SUMMARIZE (JUST THE FACTS, PLEASE)

"Sam threatened to throw your teddy in the toilet and you threw your shoe at him. Sam says he was 'just teasing' and Mary says hitting Sam with the shoe was 'an accident.'"

EXAMINE

"Mary, tell Sam how you felt when he held teddy over the toilet."
"That's my favorite teddy bear that I just got for my birthday. He wouldn't give it back." (A sob accompanies this statement.)
Offer a name for Mary's feelings. "You look very sad."
Mary nods.
"Sam, does it look like Mary was enjoying your teasing?"
"No."
"How did you feel when she threw her shoe at you?"
"It hurt. I was only playing."
"Mary, did hurting Sam make things better?"
"I guess not."
"Sam, do you think Mary knew you were playing?"

"Maybe not."

GENERALIZE

"Sam, teasing isn't fun for the person being teased. Mary, throwing things hurts others. What else could you each have done?"

This type of dialogue helps children to understand the impact of their actions, learn to name their feelings, and recognize that others have feelings, too. Sam might agree to stop teasing Mary or at least to pay attention when she gets upset. Mary could ask Sam to give her teddy bear back, seek an adult's help, or try to ignore Sam's teasing.

Does this mean that all teasing will stop or that neither child will ever hit the other again? No. This conversation or similar ones may need to be repeated many times, but over time conflicts will become less frequent; children will act more cooperatively and learn skills to process problems on their own.

LET GO

Adults need perspective, too. The squabbles over whose turn it is to carry out the trash represent relationship building, a process that is forged under stress much as steel is tempered and strengthened by heat and pressure. Learning to 'let go' shows trust in this process.

The yells coming from the back room
TODAY
represent relationships that must develop
resilience
for the times you won't be there to referee
TOMORROW.

GUESS WHAT?

Your children aren't the only ones!

Siblings aged three to seven fight as much as 3.5 times an hour, and those aged two to four — about every ten minutes!

Kluger, J.
(July 10, 2006).
"The New Science of Siblings."
Time, p. 49.

A PARENT'S SURVIVAL GUIDE
FOR SIBLING FIGHTS

REMEMBER TO:

- Choose **all** your children and love **each one best**
- Focus on **ending fights** — not **whodunit**
- **Laugh and hug** each other, often

BEFORE INTERVENING:

- Evaluate
- Stay out of the fray
- Transform your perspective

WHEN YOU MUST INTERVENE:

- Act — STOP damage
- Get everyone COOLED-OFF
- GUIDE problem-solving
- PREVENT future problems with improved SKILLS

The Parental Balancing Act

Situation: What is Fair?

*"It seems that I am always worrying about being perceived as **unfair** by my two children," says Barbara. "When I buy a souvenir for one child, I fuss to make sure I have one of equal value for the other. At Christmas I have to keep lists to be sure I give an equal number of presents to each child.*

"I need a balance scale to weigh out anything, from popcorn to peanuts, to be sure no one feels cheated. Yet no matter how careful I am — one or both complain that I've been unfair. What can I do?"

Solution: The 'Eye of the Beholder'

Fair seems to be in the 'eye of the beholder' and when that eye is looking from one sibling toward the other, the green glow of envy is pretty obvious.

Fair is not equal. This proverbial adult 'cop-out,' meant to weasel out of having to justify behavior, does nothing to allay that underlying suspicion that the adult loves a competing sibling more/better/at all!!!   If **fair** is not **equal** — why or why not?

EQUAL

Let's start with a look at **equal**. **Equal** means **the same** or at least **of the same value**. Very young children do not understand this concept because their brains cannot process it.

Piaget's concept of **conservation** explains the way a young child places more value on perceived size, i.e., five pennies spaced widely apart are going to **seem** to be **more** than the same five pennies piled together.

This means that getting a single, though expensive, doll while a younger sister gets five inexpensive coloring books — **seems unfair**. Little sister 'got more.' Explaining that the doll cost three times more than the coloring books won't help. A young child cannot understand this concept. She really can't get it.

All the adult calculations in the world will be unable to convince such a child that her single gift wasn't **less than** the multiple gifts her sister got. The brain cell development needed to understand this does not exist. Period. Don't even try.

> *"Equal — schmequal! She got more!"*

FAIR

Comprehending **conservation** does not end the problem, though. An older child who understands **conservation** may still be unhappy. Why? Because **fair** is not about **equal**.

If one child got the heirloom doll but her brother got the video game **she wanted**, it will still seem **unfair**.

> ***Equal** may be a developmental issue,*
> *but **fair** is an emotional one.*

IT HURTS

Sometimes a little commiseration can go a long way. "Mikey got the new game you wanted. It's hard to watch others play with things we wish we had, too."

"Yeah." (She heard. She cares. My feelings matter.)

The mere act of letting a child know we understand her hurt feelings can help those feelings to heal. Of course, there is nothing 'mere' about it.

NEEDS

Let's take a step away from the piles of crumpled gift-wrapping, the lamentations of ungrateful children, and the balancing scales of their well-meaning parents and look instead at **needs**.

We'll start with bedtime. Although sleep patterns will vary, most nine year olds require close to ten hours of sleep per night, while most six year olds need about eleven. Expecting both children to be in bed at the same time may be **equal** (and often quite appealing), but the **needs** of each child make an hour difference in bedtime, reasonable — and **fair**.

Will it seem **fair**? The 'eye of the beholder' will affect the answer.

If one asks the younger child, she will claim that being sent to bed first isn't **fair**, whereas if the older child does not get to stay up later, she will tell you how **unfair** that is. The simple response is, "We each need different things." This same response can be rephrased for almost any situation. Remember: Parenting decisions do not require approval ratings. Our task is to **meet needs**.

Meeting needs means different,
because needs are not the same ***or*** *equal.*

UNIQUE

If we cloned all our children, **fair** would be easy. **Equal** would rule. Alack and alas — each of them and us is **unique**. And therein lies the rub.

You are raising two or more different children, not just cookie cutter child replicas. Each will call forth **different** skills because each has **different** needs.

In *Siblings Without Rivalry* (New York: Avon Books, 1998), Adele Faber and Elaine Mazlish say "To be loved equally, is somehow to be loved less. To be loved uniquely — for one's own special self — is to be loved as much as we need to be loved." What a great way of saying it. Each of our children is **unique** just as our love for each of them will be **unique**.

WHO'S COUNTING?

Why do cries of **unfair** push your guilt button? Who is the person most worried about **equal**? Do you invite your family's manic measuring? A parent or adult who uses comparisons is setting the stage for mischief.

"Your sister never got into trouble at school." (As if this is going to make any child want to behave!)

"Why can't you sit quietly in church like your brother does?" (It is safe to assume that brother is flashing his halo while mentally snickering over this one.)

"She's our musical one. The rest of us can't carry a note!" (Speak for yourself, please!)

Comparisons invite competition.

WHO DO YOU LOVE MORE?

Maybe **more** is the wrong word here. We connect to each child in **different** ways. In the book, *I Love You the Purplest*, Barbara Joosse does a wonderful job of deflecting her sons' attempts to elicit favoritism by describing the **unique** way in which she loves each of them. "I love you the purplest" becomes a metaphor for that **uniqueness**.

*We each want to feel both loved **and** special.*

OR DO YOU?

If we do find ourselves more attuned to or comfortable with one child than another — it is time to examine our behavior for signs of **favoritism**. **Favoritism** hurts.

Once we become aware of what we are doing, we can change it.

A boisterous child can be a joy at the park or beach while your quiet and studious 'soul-mate' child will be the one to take on a stroll through a museum. Both children will feel loved and valued by being treated **differently**, whereas taking them both to the park **and** museum would open the door to comparisons, resentment and 'real or imagined' — **favoritism**.

Doing different things with each child values his or her uniqueness.

ME! ME! ME!

What is it a child is really saying when he complains that his brother got a bigger portion of potatoes? Maybe it is about the potatoes! To paraphrase Faber and Mazlish, ask, "Are you saying you are still hungry?" rather than getting out the tape measure to verify french fry length.

If one child **feels** the other is getting **more** — whether it is food, time, or attention, avoid going on the defensive or trying to rectify things to the complainer's specifications.

Acknowledge that Jimmy's science project is due tomorrow and he needs extra help right now. Offer reassurance to the other child. "I know you want me to read your new story to you. I will look forward to doing that tomorrow. Maybe you could pick out your favorite pictures and show them to me before bedtime. I'd like that."

Honest expectations, though unequal, will feel fair when presented with love — rather than apology or defensiveness.

FAIREST IN THE LAND

Years ago I had a college professor share a special way she and her husband said good night to their children. We adopted this formula and the results were wonderful. Here is how it goes:

"If you lined up all the three-year-old girls with brown curly hair in the whole, wide world, I would run up and choose you. You're the one I would want most."

"If you gathered together all the six-year-old boys with brown eyes and missing front teeth, you'd be the only one for me."

"If all the four-year-old girls with glasses were lined up in a huge, long line, I'd say, 'I want this one'."

Each of these statements would be accompanied by a BIG hug and kiss. Each child would light up with megawatts of happiness.

This formula, or any that expresses your **unique** and **special love**, promises to earn you the title of 'fairest in the land,' without the assistance of a single magic mirror, list, or tape measure.

*Finding fair may mean replacing **equal** with **unique**.*

#7

Clean-Up and Chores

Problem #7 spot is shared:
the double whammies of
CLEAN-UP and CHORES.
Let's start at the very beginning, as we
welcome baby . . .

Baby-Proofing: Baby Rules — Ready! Set! Go!

Situation: Explorer-Friendly Spaces

I have entered the magical grandparenting years, which sometimes require backtracking. Our baby granddaughter spends a lot of time at our house. We, her adoring family court, practically take numbers as we vie to hold her. The sound of her laughter, her plump cheeks, those button brown eyes — but I digress.

The point is that our dear Princess has learned to crawl. We anticipated her mobility, by moving all of the dish soap, cleansers, and carving knives to spots at adult shoulder level or higher. In spite of these precautions, our busy grandbaby was most willing to point out those few stray items that we overlooked.

There was the matter of the coils of cable cord next to the television, the sharp edge of the fireplace bricks, and of course the candies that were in the decorative can, which we did not suspect she could open. So now that our cords are hanging from the ceiling, there is a thick rug sitting lopsided in front of the fireplace, and all available containers are empty, my husband and I are reminded of the rules that brought us through the years of raising our original brood of four.

Solution
RULE # 1 — GET READY
Babies, toddlers, and preschoolers are explorers. They are also scientists, archeologists ("Oh, look, that's where my earring was!"), and animal lovers. They practice these various professions with the same restraint as a bulldozer going downhill without brakes.

At a preschool parenting class one of the parents asked, "How can I keep my child away from our home computer? How do you handle such problems here at the center?"

The center's director, who was leading the class answered, "Well, there isn't anything here they shouldn't touch. If there was, it would be out of reach." I trust that every care provider reading this could give this same answer. At home, though harder to give such an answer, it is still possible to move items out of reach. If not — look around. What needs to be changed?

A "YES-YES" PLACE
It is the life work of young children to learn about their world. Children learn through their senses. They taste:
"Hmm — cat hair, tastes nasty." Spit it out.
"Ooohh, cat food. Yum!" (Time to relocate or cover up the pet food!)

They smell, listen, and touch:
"Flowers. Nice."
"Singing. Yippee!"
"Ahhh! Warm bath."

Our job at school and home (or at grandma's) is to make sure that each experience is safe.

If yours is a "no-no" zone, then you might be standing in the way of scientific breakthroughs for that growing little brain rampaging through the room. Make your house or center a "yes-yes" place, a place for magic and discovery. There are bells hanging from my counters, to practice 'cause and effect.' We have velveteen blankets, flannel blankets, and sheep skin to crawl on, cuddle in, and keep our darling warm. The air blowing from our heater produces a look of wonder when she cruises past the vent.

Look around, notice the magic.

RULE # 2 — SET THE STAGE FOR SAFETY

It takes effort to make a "yes-yes" environment. In spite of my most magical blanket collection, the carpet creates quite a competition, especially those interesting, unidentifiable specks that fit so nicely into one's mouth. (My vacuuming schedule has quadrupled.)

The dangling phone cord is far more inviting than tinkling bells, and the call of the garbage pail can be quite compelling. Magic aside, there are still going to be dangers lurking. Young children require constant supervision. Supervision is easier when the environment is explorer-friendly.

EXPLORER-FRIENDLY

Those crystal bowls, charming collections of glass-blown frogs, or delicate ceramic roses are not bottom shelf material. As your child moves from crawling, to pulling himself up to standing position, and then to walking and climbing, the height of the family heirlooms should rise accordingly. This is now your child's home, too, and she has a brain to grow.

Fill a low kitchen drawer with pot lids, wooden spoons, and other safe utensils. Devote a cabinet to plastic bowls, pans, and toys. While you stir the gravy on the stove, your little one can stir his pots at your feet.

When he is older, he can splash away at the sink, washing the night's potatoes, readying them for baking. He can play on the floor or at a table with a basin of water and some cups and spoons (place a towel under the area to protect the floor and don't worry — kids dry off just fine), or he can enjoy the feel of warm clothes right out of the dryer as he 'helps' you fold them. Wherever you are in the house, bring your child along. If at all possible, provide an activity related to what you are doing, and both your child and his brain will thrive.

RULE # 3 — GET UP AND GO!

When it is difficult to remove something from a child's reach — try distraction. Please note that the base of that word is **action**! In other words, **get up and go**.

Distraction does not mean yelling "no-no" into outer space. Distraction means **getting up** and **going** across the room, lifting her royal highness off the keyboard, and then repositioning her in front of — the cat. (Note: This only works with extremely mellow cats capable of making fast getaways.)

"Look at Kitty's tail!"

The next minutes will pass peacefully as she forgets the computer and devotes herself to stalking the cat. (Our own cat has developed a preference for staying outside lately.)

If you don't have a congenial cat — a nice blinking rattle, pot lid and wooden spoon, or jack-in-the-box toy will work fine. Just remember that **action**, yours that is, is part of the cure.

PERSISTENCE: YOURS AND THEIRS

"What if my child persists?"

Persistence is a great life skill, but tiring in the early years. It also shows that your child is beginning to understand object permanence, another developmental plus, but a real minus for a parent's drooping energy level.

Keep at it. Swoop in, pry off those little fingers, and move her. Better yet, move the item out of her reach. If the off-limit computer can't be moved, cover it up, create a barrier, or block it off by placing a gate or small shelf in front of it.

Get ready for your explorer, set the stage for safety, and get yourself up and going — right along with that little one.

Oh dear. Excuse me, please. I believe my granddaughter just identified a potted palm that needs to be relocated to a higher shelf.

"Come with Grandma, dear. Here Kitty, Kitty!"

Reframing Your Expectations

Situation: Reframing Your View —
Changing Expectations

Thuy's problem is not her child but herself. Thuy used to pride herself on the way she kept the house; things were tidy and she would never leave even one unwashed dish in the sink.

Then her son, Thich, was born. Thich is almost two and Thuy cringes whenever someone stops by for a visit. Yesterday she was mortified when her neighbor sat down and the sofa squeaked! She tried to laugh and say, "Oh, that's where rubber ducky was hiding," but she wished she could have hidden, instead.

Thuy loves her son, but doesn't feel so great about herself anymore because she can't keep up with the mess.

Solution

Before Baby (BB) your house might have glowed with the elegance of a still life painting, but now you are living in a shifting mobile. Have your rooms taken on a fractured look as though Picasso put them together? It may be time to redefine your vision of the *Art of Homemaking*.

The changing roles of women and men have made this task extra challenging. When a child is born, we switch from being a couple, a single person, or a family of three or more. The new family configuration is an unknown. The obvious shifts of time management, responsibility, and more complex relationships are things for which we try to prepare. The less obvious shift of what we expect of others and ourselves emerges over time.

'SHOULDS' FROM THE PAST

Think of your own childhood. What did mom do? What was dad's role? What was expected of you and any siblings? Whether you choose to follow those roles or do the exact opposite, those life experiences affect your expectations.

One mom was devastated when her children turned up their noses at an elaborate strudel she had prepared. Why did she react so strongly? Images of her grandma and a warm kitchen full of spicy smells drifted through her senses. This was the strudel her grandma taught her to make. It evoked memories of the wonderful years when she and her mother had lived with her grandparents.

When her own children failed to delight in this cherished treat, she felt a sense of mourning that she could not pass her treasured childhood memories forward to her children. Realizing that the strudel represented a special memory helped her to put her children's reactions into perspective.

Such moments happen often. Tying self-worth to how well we live up to our own images of what we **should** be, how we **should** act, or what family life **ought** to be makes disappointment almost a certainty. Take a good look at what you believe you **should** be doing as a parent, wife, or husband. Then ask yourself why you think that way. What experiences led to that script in your head?

REWRITE THE SCRIPT

Now examine today. Are those expectations reasonable given your current lifestyle? If the old script doesn't work anymore, is it time to rewrite it? Let your house become a living canvas for today's family — not the remembered one in your head. Hotel room spotless might no longer fit the masterpieces living under your roof.

Before Baby, did the topic of the best way to remove mashed carrot stains from a suit jacket or the meaning to be derived from the color and consistency of baby poop ever come up? Probably not.

When you lived alone, did you think about your preference for soaking the silverware before washing it? Is it hard for you to avoid cringing each time your wife tosses an unsoaked, gravy-coated ladle into the dishwasher?

This process of redefinition involves endless minutiae. How will all this reminiscing, soul-searching, and anguish make rubber duckies in the drawing room any easier to take? That is up to you. What do you expect of yourself, your partner, and your child? What do they expect of you? What are you willing to change, let go of, or re-imagine?

HAPPIER EXPECTATIONS

You cherish the look of crisply folded linens and yet this morning you shoved the sheets into the drawer in your hurry to get to your son's preschool and take part in his turn at the program's family sharing circle. Will anyone else notice those rumpled pillowcases? Will your son notice your presence — and remember this day? Which matters more?

Use your creativity to scale down expectations to a size that will fit your family. If the soft, misty look of a Monet brings you tranquility, create a corner in your bedroom as your personal sanctuary and become more tolerant of the creative clutter in the rest of the house.

The polished look that you cultivated in your days as a single career person may keep your family at arm's length. If your arms feel lonely, then it may be time to dust those gleaming countertops with a bit of flour, hug your little one, and share her joy as she mangles bread dough, leaving a trail of floury footprints across those formerly flawless tiles.

A kitchen vibrating with bold Van Gogh colors might entice the creation of rich sauces that dribble down chins and stain collars. Give thanks for spot remover and savor these moments.

MAKE FRIENDS WITH THE MESS AND YOURSELF

Constant self-disapproval seeps into the atmosphere. It is easy for children to feel inadequate when surrounded by the muddy colors of a parent's dissatisfaction. It is equally easy to condemn a spouse who does not live up to one's vision of what **should**, **could**, or **ought to** be. Disapproval and blame do not paint pretty pictures.

REMEMBERING WHAT MATTERS

Perhaps next time the smile on your face will feel more genuine if, as you retrieve that rubber ducky, you picture your splashing toddler's joyous face. Chances are good that your neighbor will have a few rubber ducky stories of her own to share.

EMERGENCY TIPS

TIP #1:

On those days you absolutely, positively MUST dig out — pick one small area and get it in order. When it is cleared, take a short break (maybe cuddle with your child). Then tackle another small area. Each time you finish a section you will feel encouraged — and we all do better when we feel encouraged.

TIP #2:

Even a small child can help (well, sort of). Spread a towel on the floor, set out a small bowl of water, and give him a small sponge and something to scrub. The water will dry, his clothes can be changed, and he will love being near you and 'helping.'

TIP #3:

Box or bag the clutter and place it in the closet. At least things will look less overwhelming, and if guests are about to arrive — it may be your only option!

"Clean Your Room — NOW!"

Situation: "Clean Your Room — NOW!"

"You're always a meanie!" yells Marcel to Rodney's retreating back.

Surrounded by piles of dirty socks, stray copies of Dr. Seuss, and a rainbow of uncapped markers Marcel sits in his room serving out this latest time-out sentence.

The only movement likely to occur here will be Marcel flinging himself on his bed to cry; aiming an angry kick at a hapless Cat in the Hat; *or his dad, Rodney, threatening time-out extensions.*

Have you ever seen your neighbor go through this kind of struggle? (I say 'your neighbor' because this wouldn't happen in your house, right?) Well, just in case both you and your neighbor could benefit from some new strategies, read on.

Solution: What Went Wrong?

A command to "Clean your room — NOW!" has a few things going against it. First it contains the unspoken message of misery — that clear 'or suffer' threat.
'Or suffer' sounds like this: Clean your room or you — "Won't get to go

swimming"; "Visit your friend Alice"; "Watch cartoons tonight" (or ever, if one is feeling really desperate). 'Or suffer' can also sound like: Unless this mess gets cleared up in the next 10 minutes — "You will go right to bed after dinner"; "I'm taking away your new Princess doll"; "You won't be allowed to use marking pens all week."

These threats, often whitewashed with names like **consequences** or **choices**, are usually last-ditch efforts to coerce at least the appearance of cooperation. More often they are power struggles — with both parent and child locked into a battle of wills — each feeling frustrated, miserable, and equally determined, while the mess remains as immovable as they do.

WHAT DO WE MEAN?

What does 'clean your room' mean to Rodney, to Marcel, to your nattering neighbor (or even — to you)? Does Marcel think that shoving his smelly socks in the closet will get the job done, while Rodney's anticipated destination for those radioactive items is the family laundry basket?

Will tossing assorted pens and miscellaneous caps into the art drawer cover the job or do the covers need to be in place before the task is considered done?

Does your neighbor expect neatly tucked sheets and a smooth surface or does getting the pillows and blankets off the floor suffice? You may think your child knows what you expect, but often her view of the big picture is not in sync with yours.

SO BIG: WHERE TO BEGIN?

Even if your child does know what is expected — the task may feel overwhelming. Isn't it more appealing to go out to the deck to ride one's tricycle in peace than to face that room-size chaos? Wouldn't you rather watch cartoon heroines battle evil than tackle that monstrous mess on your bedroom floor?

This leads to the next problem: 'Where to begin?' which takes us back to the original communication problem — what does 'clean your room' really mean?

FRESH START

If the mess is BIG — make each task small.

Try a different starting point. "Marcel, please bring me any clothes lying on your bedroom floor."

He can do that. You can point to missed t-shirts, pajama bottoms, or stray socks and help or accompany him to carry the pile into the laundry room. This is simple, direct — and it works. On to the next step.

"There are books on the floor. Please put all of the books on the shelf." At this point your child may give you a suspicious look and ask, "Am I cleaning my room?" to which you can reply, "We're just getting things put away, dear."

PICTURE IT

A variation of this step-by-step process is to work with your child and identify all the tasks that contribute to cleaning up a mess. Make these visual by drawing images for each task or finding magazine pictures, then construct a simple chart of three to five tasks. You might have pictures of:

- a washer or box of laundry detergent
- a book or shelf of books
- a set of marking pens or a sample of your child's art

Use this visual list, asking your child what he needs to do first; then next; and so on, by referring to the images pictured.

OLDER CHILDREN

As children grow older (five and beyond, including adults!) a similar technique is to set out three labeled containers. Each container describes what goes into it:

- Put It Away (or set it aside to go to the laundry or another room)
- Give It Away (this is a great way to encourage generosity, too)
- Throw It Away (or recycle it)

All of these methods break tasks into manageable pieces, providing a clear direction out of the chaos — to order.

COMPANIONSHIP HELPS

Sometimes further resistance appears in the form of such comments as, "It's too hard"; "I'm too tired"; "There is too much to do". This is your clue to move ahead to the next strategy without losing the nice flow of cooperation.

Most of as don't like to work alone, especially if a task is not all that fun. Working together can make a job seem less daunting. Here are three ways to do this:

- ### *Offer Assistance*
"I see some markers without caps. Please bring all the markers to me and I will help you match the caps to them."

- ### *Offer to Work Together*
"I'll stack the books while you gather the markers."

- ### *Offer to Stay Nearby*
"Would you like me to stay with you while you gather your dirty clothes?"
"I'll sit here and make out our grocery list while you put your books away."

HAVE FUN

Doing a task does not have to be a misery in and of itself, either. There are ways to make it more fun for everyone. Here are a few of them:

- ### *Try a Challenge*
"Let's see who can pick up the most books."
"I'll bet I can gather all the towels from the bathroom and get them to the laundry room before you get your dirty clothes there."

- ### *Offer to Celebrate Success*
"As soon as your books are back on the shelf, let's snuggle up and read your new story."

• *Set a Team Goal*

"If we can get your room finished with enough time to get the laundry put away before lunch, we can spend this afternoon at the library."

In each of these cases, everyone comes out a winner — something missing from a power struggle. In a power struggle, someone comes out 'the winner', leaving the other with the title (often unspoken — but still felt) of 'loser.'

ATTITUDE AND GRATITUDE

Jobs of any kind play an important role in helping children to feel like valued and contributing members of the family.

Appreciation = Encouragement

Criticism = Discouragement

When we acknowledge and appreciate contributions, encouragement leads to increased cooperation. When we find fault, we get discouragement.

"You are taking good care of our marking pens. I really appreciate having them nice and moist so the colors stay bright."

Contrast that to:

"The markers got put away, but your books are still all over the floor."

Which statement would make you want to continue the job? By acknowledging one task or even a successful effort, "All but one of the marker caps is matched up. Thank you. Great job! Let's see if we can find the missing cap together," we encourage cooperation's growth.

When only perfection will do, most of us leave a lot to be desired. If perfection seems almost unattainable, why keep trying?

"CLEAN YOUR ROOM" NOT "GO TO YOUR ROOM"

The task of getting your child's (or your neighbor's child's) room cleaned does not need to end with that child being sent to her room 'to suffer.' By approaching the task in a different way, with a new attitude — the result can be cooperation as well as a clean room (or cleared up play area, de-cluttered bathroom, or the tidying up of any other mess).

Focus on cooperation instead of obedience or 'suffering'; go at it step-by-step; make the time worthwhile by expressing gratitude for your child's contributions, providing an opportunity for him to feel competent and valued.

There will be less mess and more happiness — at least at your house (though we can't guarantee what will be happening at your neighbor's).

A NEW ATTITUDE

- Focus on cooperation (not obedience)

- Give step-by-step instructions (not barked out commands)

- Express appreciation for effort (not demand perfection)

Change

Situation: A Real Journey — Not a Virtual One

"I want to change my behavior but I get really discouraged," says Ellie. "I read about a new way to get children to make their beds; stare with envy as my neighbor's kids pile into the family van without a fuss; or watch another mom tell her child 'no' in the grocery line without a tantrum resulting.

"I want those things, too, but can't seem to change my own behavior or get their dad to change his. If I do try to change, I forget and go right back to my former yelling and threatening, or begin criticizing their dad if he doesn't change, which only makes everything worse. I keep blowing it!"

Solution

Most folks don't recognize the steps involved in changing a behavior, nor do they remember that their own is the only one whose behavior they can change or control. Think of change as an action verb, rather than as a noun and don't try to make it plural. Focus on changing YOU — not the rest of the family.

Change takes place over time, through a series of steps, and with lots of mistakes along the way. Changes require new skills and skills don't come in easy-to-open, microwaveable packets, nor can they be force fed to others.

A REAL JOURNEY — NOT A VIRTUAL ONE

Think of change as a journey with recognizable signposts. Just when you feel you have gotten lost, do a compass check and you may discover that you are right on course. Let's examine this 'journey of change', while maneuvering its potholed path with a grown-up tale of: *The Real Journey to Change.*

STEP #1: Awareness

Once upon a time there was a mother, a houseful of kids, more toys than there were children, and a never-ending supply of bedtime stories. The mother's name was Mama-Droops-a-Lot.

Each evening Mama-Droops-a-Lot (MDAL) would tell her children that their toys needed to be put away before she would read bedtime stories. But alas, the blocks, markers, and puzzle pieces would remain untouched by all.

MDAL would read several stories, then stumble through the house late into the night piling blocks, re-capping markers, and hunting down missing puzzle pieces while grumbling with great bitterness.

One night MDAL noticed something. MDAL realized that she kept saying one thing, "Pick up your toys before I will read," and doing another: reading anyway. At that moment, MDAL made a vow. She would change — her behavior.

STEP #1: Awareness + Desire = Attitude Change.

STEP #2: The Announcement

The next day MDAL gathered her royal brood and told them that from now on she would only read bedtime stories after they had put their toys away.

The children were perplexed. Isn't this what she always said? They shrugged and continued slurping curds and whey. MDAL tapped her fingers. "Hmm," she thought.

STEP #2: Announcement of the intention — CHANGE AHEAD.

STEP #3: Too Late

Late that night, right after she'd finished the third bedtime story in which the valiant Prince was sent to slay a dangerous slime-eating sea monster, MDAL kissed the brows of her many sleeping children. She turned out the lights and — tripped over a tower of blocks. Up came MDAL's royal palm, ready to slap her royal forehead.

"Oh NO! Not again! I forgot," she said in a whisper (to keep from waking the children).

Dear MDAL, pray do not despair. This is no time for a slapping of foreheads. This is a time for a thumping of backs — in celebration. Why? Because MDAL had noticed! This was progress.

STEP #3: Notice after — NO CHANGE.

STEP #4: The First Stop

The castle moat turned crimson and gold as the sun set upon another day. MDAL shoved aside six teddy bears, nestled seven children under each arm, then opened the night's gilt-trimmed volume. No sooner had the captive Prince been bound and trussed than MDAL spied a stack of Lincoln logs® piled on a set of exquisite flowered tea-party china. Aha! MDAL halted with the Prince only inches from a torturer's blade.

"Okay, everybody," she said. "We forgot about picking up toys before story time. Let's see how fast we can get them put away." Her response to the grumbles that erupted was, "The sooner the job is done, the sooner the Prince gets rescued." And so everyone scurried to tidy up and in short order all was well, the Prince included.

MDAL had reached a new landmark. She stopped — then changed.

STEP #4: Notice during. Halt! Change.

STEP #5: The Road Turns

A day passed. Another night arrived: same warning; same ignoring; same beginning. MDAL was pulling out a beloved copy of *The Prince in the Dungeon* when she spotted a collapsing pillow-fort in the corner of the castle. Her royal arm halted. She slid the book back onto the shelf and said, "Toys!"

A vast silence followed. The children looked at her, then at the mess. MDAL's smile was serene as she said, "Call me when the toys are put away so that we may find out what the Prince is up to tonight," and she glided from the room. Bedlam bellowed in her wake.

STEP #5: Notice before. Halt! Changing.

STEP #6: Roadblock and Change-Back

The air was thick with whining and the gnashing of teeth. Stomping feet rattled the castle turrets. "Bring back the old Mama-Droops-a-Lot," begged the children.

But the old MDAL did not reappear. Rebellion ran rampant. Not a toy budged. When at last the new and changed Mama-Droops-Less-Often (MDLO) arrived to tuck her forlorn little ones into bed she said, "I am sure the Prince will survive an extra night in the dungeon and surely tomorrow you will remember to pick up your toys." And without another word, the new MDLO left the room, failing to rescue a single toppled pillow on her way out.

Darkness and gloom descended. The children missed the old MDLA. They sniffled into their silken pillows long into the night. No toys. No story. No happy ending to this day.

Meanwhile, a brave MDLO adjusted her earplugs and sipped golden tea in the parlor. She took heart because she recognized her children's **change-back** behavior as their attempt to get back to the 'old way' of doing things, the one they knew, thus confirming for her that her own true change had begun. Success was at hand!

*STEP #6: **Change-Back** attempts signal: Change in progress.*

STEP #7: *Staying on Course*

As MDLO helped the final child from the royal bath the next night, she realized that bedtime was only a half hour away. All thrones were buried beneath layers of dress-up scarves; a legion of crayons occupied the dining hall trestles; while assorted puzzle parts were piled up and down the marble hallways. Tonight, MDLO did not make her usual announcement. Instead she said, "What needs to be done before our story?"

By answering, the children admitted they knew. It was that simple. There was much scurrying of royal feet. Scarves, crayons, and puzzle parts flew into chests, baskets, and onto shelves. Within minutes hopeful cries of, "We're ready," rang out over the castle turrets.

MDLO smiled. She opened a book and soon the steadfast Prince discovered a field of shimmering golden daisies beneath a warm and cloudless blue sky. A meadowlark's song filled the air.

Peace reigned throughout — both kingdoms.

STEP #7: Change spreads.

STEP #8: *The Final Destination*

Weeks later, as bedtime approached, the children would hurry to shimmy into their pajamas, then dash off to replace pens into art pavilions; pile blocks into bins; and deposit bejeweled dolls into their toy cradles. Triumphant shouts of "We're ready," trumpeted across the realm.

MDLO rejoiced with her throngs of children as, at long last, the Prince won the fair Princess's heart and all lived happily ever after (or at least a bit more peacefully and with a lot less mess).

STEP #8: Change complete.

EIGHT ROAD SIGNS ON
THE ROAD TO CHANGE

- Awareness + desire = **attitude change**.
- Announcement: **Change ahead!**
- Notice after. **No change**.
- Notice during. Halt! **Change**.
- Notice before. Halt! **Changing**.
- **Change-back** attempts signal: **Change in progress!**
- **Change spreads!**
- **Change complete.**

#8

Bathroom Battles

Once again we have a tie.
Problem #8 is a double-header,
with most innings
getting played out in the bathroom.
The good news — problem #8 —
Potty Issues, is usually limited to parents of the very young.*
The sad news is that Tooth Brushing
can go on, and on, and on. . . .

NOTE:

* This does not refer to ongoing bed-wetting, which is a different issue. For help
  with bed-wetting, consult with your doctor or find help from organizations such as
  The *Hargitt House Foundation*, PO Box 130342, The Woodlands, TX 77393; or
  www.hargitthousefoundation.com or e-mail info@hargitthousefoundation.com.

Life Without Diapers

Situation: Parents Dream of Life Without Diapers

Jennifer is sick of chatting about the relative merits of cloth versus disposable diapers. She wants to banish diapers (as well as the real things) from her vocabulary altogether, but Jason won't cooperate!

His classmates wear 'big boy' clothes. He doesn't care. His drawer is filled with airplane-decorated big boy pants. He won't wear them. Jennifer sits him on the potty. He won't go — and his diaper size continues to grow!

Solution

Ah, those not so joyous potty-training days. Few of us save labels from our disposable diapers to include in Mark or Janet's baby books. Even when festooned with gala cartoon characters, tinted pastel shades of pink and blue, or sporting catchy logos — diapers are not a parent's delight.

READY OR NOT

Readiness lies at the bottom (so to speak) of toilet training troubles.
Unfortunately, mom or dad are often **ready** before their little one is.
Readiness involves three factors: physical **readiness**, emotional **readiness**, and

environmental **readiness**. Mom and dad are physically ready to pitch the diapers out the door, feeling pretty emotional about the topic, not to mention sick of living in an environment rich in potty paraphernalia. But what about Mark or young Janet?

PHYSICAL READINESS

The bladder is an inflatable organ. As children grow it becomes capable of containing larger and larger quantities. Until the bladder can handle a few hours' worth of fluid, a child has very little control over the spillover. The precursors: Those rushes of heaviness, sudden tingling, or involuntary squeezing are clues that a child needs to recognize, and then act upon (in time!).

Bowel control requires similar readiness. A child must be able to:
* hold stool
* expel stool **intentionally**
* identify early urges/body signals

Every parent recognizes that stunned, far away look young Mark gets in his eye. Sometimes a grunt or red face accompanies the moment. Usually a noticeable aroma follows close behind. In time, Mark must learn to recognize the urges that precede such moments and gallop off to the bathroom — but these things do not always occur with enough seconds to spare. With experience, timing improves.

EMOTIONAL READINESS

Emotional readiness is a bit trickier. A child determined to prove that others cannot control him may resist all **urges** (yours and his body's). The more fuss and hoopla about toileting, or increased pressure to perform, the more likely toilet training will stall.

Another reason for toileting setbacks may be a child's unwillingness to leave behind the 'specialness' of babyhood. This is particularly true when a new sibling enters the family. A child previously potty trained may revert to diapers in a bid to regain some of the attention he had before the baby arrived.

Any change in the family situation might have a similar delaying effect or reverse previous successes. A move, a new preschool, or a house full of visiting relatives may precipitate toileting problems. Parents separating, getting divorced or remarried, or simply dating again might be additional contributing factors.

One toddler made her attitude clear after her family's move to a new house. While the others unpacked, she grabbed the arm of her potty-chair, dragged the whole thing across the room and shoved it out the door. Hmm . . . a rather clear message!

REASSURE
First, be sure your child is not afraid of being swallowed by the toilet. Let him flush the toilet and watch the process. Help him see that he is too big to fit down the toilet. (If this remains a problem, wait until he has left the bathroom to flush the toilet, at least until he feels safer.)

RETREAT
Don't make toileting into a battle. Stay matter-of-fact. Mention how great you feel after using the toilet or say, "Uh-oh, I need to go to the bathroom to pee," (or whatever word(s) your family considers appropriate for such functions). Make bathroom use everyone's business — in that we all 'do it.'

Focus on helping your child adjust to possible changes. Don't worry about toileting setbacks. Once the emotional situation is addressed, the toileting will get back on track without much fuss.

ENVIRONMENTAL READINESS
Awareness is critical to success. If at all possible, especially on warm days, allow a child to go diaper-free. This could mean simply bare-bottomed, or if that feels uncomfortable to you, dress your child in a unisex smock that camouflages the lack of a diaper underneath. (Ideally we are talking about doing this in a nice grassy yard or at least on an uncarpeted surface, with plenty of disinfecting clean-up supplies handy.) The discovery of her own bodily functions in this 'natural' state will go a long way towards helping a child 'catch on' to the process. She can see

what is taking place, making it much easier to explain exactly what you want her to do in the bathroom as you clean up those puddles on the floor.

Most disposables marketed for this transition time allow a child to **feel wet** which also raises awareness. (Tip: Consider referring to these as Pull-Downs, instead of Pull-Ups®, since getting them down is the crucial consideration here.)

Watching mom or dad serves this same purpose, but if this represents more togetherness than you bargained for, do only what feels acceptable to you.

THREE Cs

The final environmental factors are those of **capability, convenience,** and **comfort**. Evaluate the environment. Is your child **capable** of pulling down or removing his pants? Does there need to be a smaller toilet seat or potty-chair for more **convenient** access? Is your bathroom a **comfortable** place in which to spend time?

• *Capability*

The sudden urge to use the toilet leaves little time to dawdle. If it takes you five minutes to get little Anna into her cute lacy tights and pantalets, she probably won't get them down in time to hop onto the toilet.

• *Convenience*

If Mark needs to drag a stool from his bedroom to the bathroom to climb up high enough to take aim, he is pretty likely to be off target.

• *Comfort*

Keeping a few children's books in the bathroom provides a comfortable setting. Looking at them might help a child stay seated long enough to get the job done.

SUCCESS AT LAST

Be sure to include lessons in good hygiene, such as hand washing (see box), toilet flushing, and how to hold the toilet paper (as well as how much to use). When physical, emotional, and environmental readiness combine, toilet training will succeed.

Parents and children will eventually get their readiness in sync. The day will truly come when diapers are forgotten memories.

Final Reminder:

Adults can set the stage for toileting success,
but it is the child who performs.

TIP: A consolation as those diaper days drag on . . . biodegradable disposables do exist and with babies going through around 30,000 disposables a minute (just in America) that news is good for all of us. Check out www.gdiapers.com, for more information or check the web and local stores as more versions become available.

HANDWASHING HYGIENE TECHNIQUE

DEMONSTRATE THE DETAILS:

- Roll or push up sleeves
- Wet hands
- Pump a drop of soap onto the palms of the hand or wet a bar of soap and rub it between the hands
- Lather up
- Optional: Make up a silly song to sing that will last about 10 seconds, the length of time it takes to kill E. Coli bacteria
  (i.e., Twinkle, twinkle wiggly worms
  Wash away the dirt and germs
  Make my hands all clean and bright
  Shiny as the morning light.)
  (No one said it has to be something that will get nominated for a Grammy!)
- Rinse thoroughly, rubbing hands under running water
- Dry hands well
- Use towel to turn off tap
- All done!

Sparkling Teeth Without Sparking a Battle

Situation: To Brush or Not to Brush (and How???)

"Our dentist insists that I brush my daughter's teeth," says Mike, *"but it has become increasingly impossible as she gets older. She is now four and last night I actually squeezed her jaw to force her to open her mouth.*

"I felt ashamed of myself. I know that I have to protect her teeth with proper brushing, but I hate these daily battles. It seems we fight over just about everything."

Solution

As you squeeze you daughter's jaw, chase her down the hall, or whatever else it takes to get that toothbrush inside her mouth, ask yourself, "Just what bad thing am I trying to prevent here?" Tooth decay???

I know teeth are vital, I use mine all the time, but I truly believe I would enjoy them a whole lot less if I had to spend much of my energy clamping them shut to prove that I was in control. The battles you describe are about power, not teeth.

POWER STRUGGLES/BELIEFS

When children are forced into compliance, they begin to believe that they must prove to the world that no one can make them do anything. This forms part of their belief system, and beliefs are potent forces.

Let's examine power struggles. Here are some **power struggle** truths:

- Struggles require resistance
- Choices invite cooperation
- Winners require losers

STRUGGLES REQUIRE RESISTANCE

Try pushing your hand against the wall — good and hard. The wall offers resistance. Now remove your hand from the wall, but keep pushing. Poof! Nothing. Without resistance, the struggle ceases.

Power struggles take two, so whose behavior can you control? Stop being the wall! When your daughter plants her feet in defiance, leave the room and request that she let you know when she is ready to cooperate. "Fine!" you say. "She will be delighted and nothing will get done."

Actually she will probably be astonished, if not struck dumb that you have changed the script. "You can't make me!" she might taunt as she shadows you into the next room. Do not respond. Just this much — this breaking of the usual power struggle dynamic — will make a huge difference.

Once an old pattern is broken, there is room for growth.

Let's apply this to tooth brushing. Your daughter is gloating, maybe even twirling the toothbrush as a makeshift baton to get you engaged. You rearrange the shampoo bottles, or maybe brush your own teeth, even hum to yourself. Of course, you may be thinking, "This is stupid. This idea is not going to work. Her teeth will fall out. Everyone will think I am a wimp. I am not sure I can keep from screaming if she drops that toothbrush one more time!" And yet — you continue not to respond.

Congratulations! You have achieved step #1 of your three-step plan to eliminate power struggles: you managed self-control; didn't push back — thereby removing resistance.

CHOICES AND COOPERATION

When we invite children to help solve problems, they are much more likely to cooperate. The key here is the word **invite**. We invite people to parties, to dinner, or to the movies. Sometimes they decline. If your friend says, "No thanks" when you invite her to a movie, do you show up and duct tape her to the car or carry her fireman-style over your shoulder into the theater? Hopefully not. "But," you say, "my friend's teeth aren't rotting in place."

Well, if you can't live with the idea of actually **inviting** cooperation, at least offer limited choices. Choices feel good. We all like to have some say in what we do. If your friend agrees to go to the movies this weekend, maybe she could at least choose the movie.

Let's look at possible tooth-related choices. "Do you want to put the toothpaste on the brush or do you want me to?" That is a nice choice. It implies that tooth brushing is a given.

Or perhaps try, "Would you like to have your teeth brushed before or after bath time?" Another healthy choice, again making the actual tooth brushing non-negotiable.

By focusing on appropriate (limited) choices, the struggle over whether to brush or not is extracted, roots and all.

Choices turn challenges into cooperation.

WINNERS AND LOSERS

Power struggles are win-lose contests. Was raising a 'loser' ever part of your long-range vision as a parent? The key here is to get to situations that are win-win. Win-win means everyone feels good about the outcome.

You asked your daughter to let you know when she was ready to cooperate. For the past two nights the toothbrush has remained in a pristine state of disuse. Let's look for some win-win options.

The first and best one usually involves working with the child to devise a solution. Admit that you are worried about her teeth, but that you do not want to fight over tooth brushing anymore. Then ask if she is willing to help you come up with a better plan.

Children love to help and have great imaginations.

Be ready to listen, stay curious, and do not find fault with every suggestion she makes. Look for a win-win solution.

She wants to brush without your help. Make that part of the plan. Suggest that she brush alone after breakfast and that she start the job at bedtime, then allow you to help her finish each night. She will feel empowered, listened to, and competent. You won't have to save up for her future dentures and can breathe easily when she flashes her sparkling choppers at the dentist.

Another solution might be to trade favors. She gets to brush your teeth while you brush hers, turning this time into shared fun, laughter, and intimacy rather than the daily wrestling match.

These are just possibilities. Figure out solutions that work for both of you. That is win-win!

HEALTHY TEETH

Of course healthy teeth are important, but there are plenty of ways to achieve stunning smiles **and** healthy self-esteem at the same time. Seattle pediatric dentist Dr. Steven Smutka offers these tips. He recommends that parents begin brushing from the appearance of the child's first tooth (about four to six months of age). "Use a soft brush and make tooth brushing a daily habit."

He adds that positioning is important. Once your child is able to stand, allow her to watch in the mirror so that she can see what is going on, thus positioning yourself so you can see into her mouth, as well.

Tooth brushing is also a dexterity issue. It is hard for children to maneuver the toothbrush and keep at it for the recommended two minutes. At about age five, consider getting a child size electric toothbrush to improve your child's efficiency at this task. Some even have timers.

PREVENTION

Actual tooth brushing is only one aspect of dental health. Follow wise eating habits: without candy, sugary sodas, or chewing gum, teeth are more likely to flourish. Offer an apple for a bedtime snack instead of a sugary cookie. Grow healthy teeth from the inside out.

Healthy teeth and power struggles need not be clamped together. Remove resistance as well as plaque; offer choices instead of challenges; and let your child's winning smile signal success for a family of winners.

#9 and #10

The Top Ten Preschool Parenting Problems

*At this point, we move from
defiance to flat-out provocation
(or at least what most adults interpret as such)
with problem #9 (Hurting Behaviors)
and problem #10 (Potty Talk and Bad Language).
Whether children mean to be hurtful,
are feeling frustrated or hurt themselves,
or simply want attention —
these behaviors get us in the gut.*

#9

Hurting Behaviors

Problem #9 involves things that
'ting' — the Hurting Behaviors.
Included are hit-ting, spit-ting, bi-ting,
and kick-ing or pinch-ing (no 'ting', but close).
Let's take a look.

Dinosaur Day Camp:
What To Do When Children
Hit, Kick, Pinch, Spit

Situation: Dinosaur Day Camp:
Hitting, Kicking, Pinching, Spitting . . .

Adults say:

"Did you push Johnny down?"

"You cannot spit at your sister!"

"Mikey's your friend. How could you pinch him?"

Children's real answers (if they could say them):

"Yep!"

"But I just did."

"Here, I'll show you how it's done."

Solution: It Isn't About Size

Have you ever heard or made statements like these? Hitting, pushing, pinching, or kicking are upsetting, and spitting really invites outrage. But the truth is that when one child hurts another, both children suffer and neither is able to listen or do much thinking about it. Why? Welcome to Dinosaur Day Camp . . .

DINOSAUR DAY CAMP

Children must learn to play with others, share, and control their impulses. We all know what it feels like to want to wallop someone (even if we only admit it to ourselves), but as adults our brain development (hopefully) allows us to control these impulses.

Children's brains and bodies are still growing and the part of their brains that work best early on is the part in charge of instincts, basic survival, and nonverbal communication — a.k.a. the Dinosaur Brain. So let's imagine a day at Jolly Jurassic Preschool.

Baby Brontosaurus hums as she digs in the sandbox, then as soon as she sets her shovel aside, T. (for toddler) Rex thunders over to grab it. In a flash the humming stops as Baby Brontosaurus flips her tail and whacks T. Rex on the side of the head. T. Rex opens his jaws and lunges forward, ready to clamp onto Baby B's tender neck. They both want that sand shovel and the earth will tremble as they grapple for it.

With this silly image in mind, let's turn to the real world of toddlers and preschoolers as they develop both their brains and a few social skills. Depending upon the child's age, we will need to adjust our responses, but there are some basic principles that apply to all:

• *Damage Control*

Under age two, a child often needs to be picked up and relocated. There is no point in a discussion. We need to get these two apart before T. Rex's jaws can connect with the target.

After age three, a child may chose to walk on his own or be given the option of being led away. If he refuses to do so, then we need to lead the injured child to safety. No matter the age (Jurassic, toddler, or kindergartener), this initial separation is basic Damage Control.

Damage Control: The first response when one child hurts another.

• Dress Wounds

Damage is seldom confined to physical wounds. Emotional wounds often precede or result from one child hurting another. Young dinosaur-thinkers use their bodies to communicate:

"That's mine!" becomes a grab.
"Let go!" becomes a shove.
"Move out of my way!" turns into a punch or kick.
"That hurts!" transforms into a pinch.
"I'm scared," "I am angry," or "Let me play, too," turns into a push, pulled hair, or a tumbled block tower.

So, when your little Stegosaurus bops a playmate — pull them apart (damage control) and then tend to wounds. Patch-up owies and dry everyone's tears.

> *Dress Wounds: Patch up physical wounds,*
> *and then work on patching-up relationships*
> *(after tempers have a chance to Cool Down).*

• Delay/Cool Down

We all need time for overheated emotions to Cool Down. This delay allows a few brain cells to re-engage. When human brains become submerged in the chemical soup produced by strong emotions, logical thinking ceases. Delay provides that necessary recovery interval.

> *Delay/Cool Down:*
> *Give tempers time to cool and brains time to resume functioning.*

• Dissect Details

Follow this Cool Down period with a Dissection of Details. What happened? Who did what? To whom? Then what? If children are too young to talk, ask questions that outline the situation and only require nods of agreement:

"Was Billy playing with the truck?"

"Did you want to use it?"
"Did you push Billy?"
"Billy, did you pinch Mary?"

With older children, give each one a chance to tell her version of the story (without interruptions or corrections). Confirm what is said and move the story forward with questions:

"Evie pushed you off the swing. Then what happened?"
"Ramona, you pulled Evie's hair after she pushed you. Is that right?"
"Tell me more about that."

Next, point out that things did not go well for either of them:

"Are either of you playing on the swing right now?"
"That's right, you aren't on the swings because you both got sent inside."

Dissect, detail by detail. Name feelings as they are uncovered and offer appropriate ways to express them:

"Ramona, you look sad. You can use your words to say, 'I feel sad.'"

> *Dissect Details:*
> *Gather details. Dissect what happened.*
> *Decide what went wrong. Name feelings.*

• Different Decisions
With both younger and older children, explain what is expected, offer alternatives, and pantomime better choices with them:

"We need to use gentle touches."
"It's more fun when we share things. Let's try taking turns pushing the truck to one another."
"Let's put this toy away for now and find something different to play with."

Pinpoint what went wrong, using questions to keep both children involved in the discussion. Explore different (and more acceptable) decisions:

"What can we do instead of pushing someone off when we want to use the swing?"
"Yes, asking for a turn is a much better decision."

Repeat the rules:

"It is still not okay to push, pull hair, or hurt others, even when we feel sad or upset."

Different Decisions:
Explore and identify different decisions that will improve
future outcomes. Repeat rules.

• Dress Rehearsal
To perform well, children need practice — and that means repetition. Role-play is a great tool for practicing new skills. Over time these practice performances will turn into polished skills that children will master and use in daily life. At first props may be needed. Use hand puppets, dolls, and teddy bears (these are especially helpful for younger children) to act out new scenes:

"Bobby, pretend that you are teddy and Mary, you hold bunny."
"Bobby, will you show us how teddy can hand the truck to bunny when he is through playing with it?"
"Now Mary, will you help bunny say, 'thank you' to teddy?"

Redo similar scenes with older children (with or without props). Set up each scene in advance:

"Let's practice asking to use the swing."
"Evie, please show us how to ask for a turn on the swing."

Prompt players as needed:

"If you are still using the swing, Ramona, what could you say to Evie?"
Ramona: "I'm still using it. I'll be done in five minutes."

Be an appreciative audience and applaud performances:

"That was a very nice way to ask. Thank you both for showing us how to ask for turns."

Dress Rehearsal: Set up opportunities to practice new skills and acceptable responses. Offer prompts. Applaud progress.

TAKE IT 'D' BY 'D'

With understanding, time, and practice, all children can evolve into the delightful, polite, and cooperative youngsters we look forward to them becoming.

DINOSAURS-IN-TRAINING
TAKE IT 'D' BY 'D'

- **Damage Control:** The first response when one child hurts another.
- **Dress Wounds:** Patch up physical wounds, and then work on patching up relationships (after tempers have a chance to cool down).
- **Delay/Cool Down:** Give tempers time to cool and brains time to resume functioning.
- **Dissect Details:** Gather details. Dissect what happened. Decide what went wrong. Name feelings.
- **Different Decisions:** Explore and identify different decisions that will improve future outcomes. Repeat rules.
- **Dress Rehearsal:** Set up opportunities to practice new skills and acceptable responses. Offer prompts. Applaud progress.

"No Hitting!"

Situation: "No Hitting" — This Applies to Everyone

One parent told me that whenever she sees a new parenting book, she turns to the index and looks up 'hitting'. "Those that do list it refer to spanking or children fighting," she said. "My problem is my son hitting me. Our son is four and when he gets angry, he hits his father and me. He kicks, shoves, and pushes us. When this happens, we are stunned and don't know what to do. We don't spank him; we are non-violent people; and we never argue in front of him. How can we help him get rid of his anger and stop his hitting?"

Solution: Not Dominoes

Anger and hitting are not the same. Anger is a feeling and hitting is an action. When your son has just kicked you in the shin, this may seem like a meaningless distinction. But it is an important difference because it shifts attention from the anger, which we can't eliminate, to the hitting, which we can.

Everyone feels angry at times. Most of us, unless we are about to be canonized, are likely to admit to having been angry, irritated, frustrated, or annoyed in the past seven days of our lives. Whether upset over the two-and-a-half hour wait at the doctor's office; riled at the phone company's latest overcharges; or steamed because raspberry jam dripped onto a new white shirt doesn't matter. Anger is anger.

Our thoughts trigger feelings: the doctors must all be in the back room playing video games; the phone company computer is out to get me; or I am a total klutz. Though our thoughts might kick-start feelings, kicking is an action and we choose our actions. They are not inevitable.

Thoughts, feelings, and actions do not need to tumble into one another like a row of dominoes whenever the first one in line gets tapped.

IMPULSE CONTROL

The younger we are, the closer together our thoughts, feelings, and actions are. Children must learn to separate their actions from their thoughts and feelings. This is called 'impulse control' and many of us, as adults, still find it difficult to do.

KEEP THINGS 'UNDER CONTROL'

When a child hits you — get his attention. State the rule. "No hitting." Be clear about what is acceptable. It doesn't help to say it while doing it, though. Spanking a child while saying, "No hitting," sends a double message. The words say one thing while our actions say another. Which do you think speaks louder? Go beyond saying (or doing) what you don't want and describe what you do want:

"Use a kind voice."
"Keep toys on the floor."
"Be gentle when you touch others."

At some point one of you may need a time-out. I say 'one of you' because it may be more effective to walk to your own room, close the door, and listen to the pounding coming from the other side of the door than to wrestle fifty-plus pounds of flailing child to his room.

Either way, removing one of you from the room separates the hitter from the hittee, which stops the hitting.

SHOW AND TEACH SELF-CONTROL

If we don't show children how to handle anger, how will they learn? Seething unspoken anger, hostile silences, and embalmed smiles may teach children to hide or try to deny their own anger.

If one parent yells at the other, the person being yelled at can say that he or she wants to be spoken to in a respectful voice. If the yelling continues, leave the room with dignity, thus modeling both self-control and self-respect.

What if your neighbor comes by to tell you to keep your dog, Angus, out of her pansies, calling Angus some unfavorable names in the process? After she returns to her side of the street, you explain to little Joey, who is clutching the miscreant Angus to his chest and listening wide-eyed, that you are feeling upset. Give Angus a scratch between the ears and take some deep breaths to calm yourself.

You don't need to say that you are upset in the same voice that you might murmur 'thanks' to an usher in a darkened theater. If your voice goes up a notch or two, that is fine. Using that notched-up voice to tell your neighbor what you think of her cats, on the other hand, would not have been so fine.

Remember, little Joey is watching **and** learning.

WHAT'S IT ALL ABOUT?

Often anger covers up other feelings. Siobhan worried about her daughter Elana's recent yelling and spitting. With Elana's aunt in the hospital, Siobhan found Elana's new behavior even more distressing. It never occurred to Siobhan to connect Elana's spitting with her aunt's illness. Not wanting to frighten Elana, Siobhan had tried not to speak of it. But children see, and hear, and think.

Elana had seen her mother crying and drawn her own conclusions. Because she couldn't put her feelings into words Elana didn't say, "I am scared. I am sad. I am worried Auntie will die." Instead Elana pulled her brother's hair, spit at her mom, and threw her lunchbox.

When Siobhan realized the connection between Elana's actions and her aunt's illness, she made time to talk about it. Siobhan told Elana that she was feeling sad, scared, and worried about Auntie, too.

By giving names to these feelings, Siobhan gave Elana words and permission to express her own feelings. Elana's spitting ended. She made her aunt pictures and wrote her notes for the duration of her hospital stay; both actions that helped Elana handle her feelings.

PREVENT THE 'OUT-OF-CONTROL'

Can you guess when your child will be most vulnerable to anger? Is he fed, rested, and at ease? A hungry or thirsty child has a greater chance of feeling overwhelmed by a side trip to the post office.

A tired child is unlikely to handle the loss of his favorite stuffed bear with much perspective. Prevent things from getting out-of-control by staying alert to your child's needs.

REIN IT IN

What helps your child calm down: holding his hands; hugging him; or giving him time by himself? Is he throbbing with unused energy? Would running, playing tag, or chasing a ball help? Does snuggling with a book, playing soft music, or dancing improve things?

Use what has worked in the past to help in the future. Involve your child in such plans. Help him think of ways to release the energy of angry feelings with actions that don't hurt others: jumping on a trampoline, drawing an angry picture, or squeezing play dough.

HEAD IT OFF AT THE PASS

Teach children how to corral feelings before they gallop out-of-control with a bit of horse sense. Harness run-away emotions; slow 'em down; and round 'em up.

• *Harness run-away emotions by establishing a breathing pattern:*
  Breathe in: 1-2-3
  Hold it: 1-2-3
  Breathe out: 1-2-3
  Pause: 1-2-3
  Repeat

• *"Whoa, back!" Slow down the action.*
  Tap one finger at a time to a knee while counting to ten.

• *"Round 'em up!" Combine visualizing, counting, and breathing.*
  Hold each breath for a count of three while picturing the corners of an imagined square (or corral), mentally moving from one corner to the next with each inhalation or exhalation.

CONTROL ISSUES

We can't control angry feelings, but we can learn acceptable ways to prevent and control angry actions:

• **Model and Teach 'Self Control'**
  Name feelings
  Discuss and model acceptable ways to express feelings

• **Keep Things 'Under Control'**
  Be clear; say what you want
  Stop further damage (take your own time-out, if need be)

• **Prevent the 'Out-of-Control'**
  Keep alert to your child's needs
  Identify, teach, and practice calming techniques

To Spank or Not to Spank

Situation: To Spank or Not to Spank —
and What to Do Instead?

The cartoon showed a maitre d' greeting a family, the toddler pulling his mother's hair, and the preschooler tugging her hand. The caption read: "Would you prefer the spanking or non-spanking section?"

When I first saw that cartoon, I despaired that we were destined for the spanking section with our ketchup-spilling, table-crawling, sugar packet-collecting brood of four. We did manage to civilize our kids and stay seated in the non-spanking section, but it didn't come naturally.

Solution

We all want to help our children. We really do. The question is how to do it? In the book *Anger*, Mitch Messer, Roman Coronado-Bogniak, and Linda Dillon write, "We learn anger management the same way we learn to wash dishes and make beds . . . (we) adopt a mannerism that will last a lifetime. In other words, in the area of anger management, there hasn't been a brain cell working for four generations."

Replace **anger management** with the word **spanking** and the same statement fits. Little Bobby pulls his sister Susie's hair and Bobby's father Jim gives Bobby the same swat his mother, Grandma Rose, used to give Jim for pulling his sister Margo's hair. Jim also forgets that he still tugs on Margo's now gray-streaked hair, just as he used to yank her braids years ago, in spite of those long ago paddlings.

Perhaps it is time to get some new brain cells working.

NOT HARMFUL DOESN'T MEAN DESIRABLE

One research report from the Institute of Human Development at the University of California, Berkeley, made headlines by saying that **mild spanking** would not hurt a child's social or emotional growth. We could ask, "What is **mild**?" But the question itself identifies what most adults fear: will an intended **mild** swat on the bottom turn into a stinging red welt, a bruised hip, or worse? When does **mild** become **too much**?

Instead of trying to define what is **mild** or how much is **too much**, why not ask a different question? What does spanking accomplish? We know what we want it to do: change behavior. But does it? Just ask Jim or Margo.

INTERRUPT OR CHANGE?

Do you ever feel like a rerun of your own movie? Yesterday you yelled at Marty for calling his brother a 'doo-doo head', spanked him, and sent him to his room. Today Marty is back in his room — same reason, new spanking. What do you think the odds are for reruns of Marty's name-calling and your spanking? Higher than you wish? Why? The answer is simple: spanking is better at interrupting misbehavior than at changing it.

SLOW LEARNERS

Years ago, whenever we opened our front door, our dog Squeaker would race outside to chase the neighbor's cat. One spring the neighbors, and therefore their cat, moved. Months (years, in fact) later, Squeaker was still tearing outside in eager pursuit of the former resident cat, and he kept at it, even though he never saw that cat again.

Sometimes we keep doing the same thing over and over expecting the result to change. Has your cat moved? Do you keep spanking even though the name-calling (or some other misbehavior) doesn't change?

THE HAND AND THE BAG

Picture a paper bag; inside that sack repose all of the tools, tricks, and teachings we call **discipline**. Some bags are lightweight, some rattle a bit when shaken, and a few bulge with possibilities. But no matter how little or how much the bags contain, the same thing happens when they are empty. We reach inside, our hand zigzags back and forth, and our fingers fail to detect anything there — until, with a final lunge, we rip through the bottom.

The hand that emerges from that empty bag of discipline tools is the hand that spanks.

Does your tool bag leave you empty-handed? Spanking is, at best, a last resort and at worst, the ONLY tool in the bag.

DOESN'T TEACH

Lilly's job involved doing home visits at a nearby military base. Each week she would spend an hour or two in a family's home. As women nursed their newborns, Lilly would stir pots of bubbling stew, serve up juice and crackers to toddlers, or fold diapers still warm from the dryer, while listening to each young mother's concerns and worries.

In mid-October Lilly was sharing an overstuffed sofa beside a mom whose sixteen-month-old daughter played nearby. As they chatted, the child kept busy by pushing a chair across the floor to the television console and scaling to the top of the set. When her mom saw what the child had done, she hurried across the room, yanked the would-be mountaineer off the television, and swatted her bottom.

"No! No! Bad girl! You can't climb up there."

Well, she had climbed up there, thought Lilly, uncomfortable seeing the toddler spanked, but not knowing what she could say or do without losing the mother's trust.

By Lilly's next visit, fallen leaves formed a colorful nest for the grinning jack-o-lantern stationed on the family's front steps. Lilly joined the mom in the living room, as before, and within ten minutes the toddler was again standing on top of the television set. This time Lilly hurried to lift the child down, holding out a book she had brought with her. The toddler forgot her climbing expedition and settled into Lilly's lap, pointing to the pictures as she helped turn the cardboard pages.

"I guess the spanking didn't teach her to stop climbing, did it?" Lilly said.

The mom sighed, nodding in agreement, "No, spanking doesn't stop her." Why not?

Spanking doesn't teach.

TO DO OR NOT TO DO

Why do we spank? It comes down to a simple equation: we either want children to do something or not to do something:

"Pick up your toys."
"Quit throwing the crayons."

Have you ever noticed that the toys still keep appearing where you don't want them to or some new variation appears? Does crayon throwing end this afternoon but reappear at dinnertime as tossed noodles, at bedtime as a flying shoe, or at the park as an upended bucket of sand?

If we want the toys to get picked up (day after day), or the throwing to stop (and not restart), then we need to switch tools.

PAST, PRESENT, AND FUTURE

If your parenting tool bag is torn and ragged, leaving you empty-handed, it may be time to retrain some brain cells, take a seat in the non-spanking section, and keep your hands to yourself. The fastest way to a future that promises your child's improved behavior could just be to change your own.

The E.P.A. (Encouragement/Prevention/Action) plan described on the next page, offers some em**power**ing tools for that discipline tool bag to keep it plump with possibility and prevent those punishing hands from escaping.

E.P.A.

ENCOURAGEMENT/PREVENTION/ACTION

TOOLS THAT WORK — CHANGES THAT LAST

Problem   Block throwing

Encouragement

- Acknowledge   "You are keeping the blocks on the floor."

  "You made your blocks into a circle."

- Appreciate   "You are treating the blocks with care."

  "Thank you for keeping the blocks on the play rug."

Acknowledgement and appreciation encourage repetition.

Prevention

- Clear expectations/

  Limits   "We need to keep all of the blocks on the

  carpeted part of the floor."

  "Blocks must stay on the ground."

- Model   "Let's see how high we can build this tower."

Problems that don't happen — don't need to be solved.
That's prevention!

Action

- State what you

  will do: "If there is any block throwing, I will take the

  blocks away."

- Follow-through   If you say it, do It.

  When a block goes sailing through the air,

  remove the blocks (without saying a word).

Control your actions and — they'll learn to control theirs.

Living With a Munchkin:
A Look at Biting

Situation: What To Do About Biting

"My sixteen-month-old daughter bit two children at her child care last week," said Alison. *"She seems to bite when she is frustrated. My mother says to bite her back, but that seems crazy to me. Her dad says a spanking will grab her attention, but I really don't want to hit her. Time-out doesn't seem to have any effect. The problem is I don't know what else to do. I am afraid she will be kicked out of child care if her biting continues. How can I stop her biting?"*

Solution

When the subject of biting comes up, parents avert their eyes and child care teachers get a cornered look. We're horrified when a little one turns tear-filled eyes towards us, while holding up an arm marked with an arc of tiny red indentations. Anger towards the biter sizzles, with punishment close behind.

There seem to be two categories of biting. The largest category consists of biting from about fourteen months to three years. The second category is the biting which occurs from the late preschool years onward.

In the first instance, biting corresponds to developmental stages. This first type of biting comprises the remainder of this chapter. The second type of biting has lots more variables. When older children bite, the reasons may relate to delays in impulse control, other biological or environmental conditions, or lagging social skill development. For these reasons, I encourage families with older biters to seek additional help, including a thorough speech and hearing evaluation.

Whatever the type of biting, one thing is certain: biting sets everyone's teeth on edge.

A DEVELOPMENTAL STAGE

The good news is that your toddler will probably outgrow her biting soon. The bad news is that it probably won't seem soon enough.

Your wisdom exceeds grandma's this time. Biting your daughter back will not teach her to quit biting. There will just be two of you biting instead of one. Your husband's spanking solution promises to create a new and even more lasting problem. Today's research confirms that children who are hit, learn to hit. Instead of biting, will your daughter progress to hitting?

Other common tactics include washing a child's mouth out with soap or placing bitters or hot sauce on the tongue, all of which border on abusive.

Bottom line: biting back, spanking, or filling a child's mouth with soap do not eliminate biting. There really are no quick fixes to stop biting, but there are several things that will help.

LANGUAGE DEVELOPMENT AND TRAINING

Early biting usually relates to language development. A child can't say she is upset, so she bites. She might feel angry, tired, or sad, but she does not know how to tell one feeling from another. Children need to recognize and learn how to articulate feelings.

Talk about the feelings a child encounters. Use books to help with this: "Baby raccoon looks very tired. Have you ever felt tired? Remember how your eyes start to close? That is what 'tired' can feel like."

Another way to teach about feelings is to use a teddy bear, doll, or even the family poodle:

"How does teddy act when he feels angry? Should teddy stomp his feet and hit the other toys? Would it help if teddy took time to cool off when he gets mad? We can cool off, too, when we get mad."

"How does Daisy Doll feel when her mommy goes to work in the morning? I'll bet she feels sad. Do you feel sad when mommy goes to work? It would be okay for Daisy to cry. We can cry when we feel sad, too."

"What happens when Patsy our poodle feels afraid? She barks and makes lots of noise, doesn't she? What can you do when you feel afraid? Would it help to ask for a hug?"

In each case, notice that a specific acceptable action is always included.

CENTER OF THE UNIVERSE

During her first three years a child sees herself as the 'center of the universe'. She may get upset and bite because she didn't get the sand bucket she wanted, but she does not realize that her biting hurts others. Others are not part of her universe.

Making her sit and **think** about her behavior is fruitless. She cannot think about things outside this known universe, which happens to consist of her.

EXPECT THE POSSIBLE

Expect your child to be developmentally her age. A 'center of the universe'-thinking toddler needs experiences appropriate to her abilities. Because sharing is difficult, minimize her need to share.

Set out several sets of blocks or as many glue sticks as there are children. At the same time, provide early sharing practice by giving her two cookies: one for herself and one to hand to her playmate. These fit her abilities.

OTHER POSSIBILITIES

One recent theory that has been proposed is that early biting is tied to the development of a child's oral needs, especially the need to chew. When biters were given chewy foods such as bagels or raisins, foods to suck such as orange wedges, or things that crunch such as graham crackers and rice cakes, their biting incidents reduced. (For more on this, including a chart of food suggestions please refer to "A New Bit on Toddler Biting: The Influence of Food, Oral Motor Development, and Sensory Activities" (see adjacent box.)

Prevention begins with observation. When, where, or whom does your daughter bite? Is it:

Toddler Oral Motor Development Food List

Foods to suck
grapefruit/orange wedges
juices
yogurt smoothies
milkshakes
frozen juice bars
gelatin cubes
applesauce
pudding

Foods to gum/munch/crunch
apple slices
blueberries
banana chunks
whole-grain crackers
rice cakes
graham crackers
oat O's cereals
soft tortilla strips
tofu cubes
raw vegetable slices
salt-free pretzels

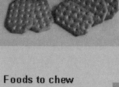

Foods to chew
jerky
cheese cubes/slices
bagels
raw veggies (zucchini, mushrooms, lettuce leaves)
tender meat tidbits
raisins
oranges

Foods to provide sensory stimulation
salsa
ice chips
lemon wedges
cinnamon sticks

Ramming, P., C.S. Kyger, & S.D. Thompson. (2006). A new bit on toddler biting: The influence of food, oral motor development, and sensory activities. *Young Children, 61*(2): 17-23. Reprinted with permission from the National Association for the Education of Young Children.

At a certain time of day?

At a certain place?

With a particular child or adult?

What else is going on?

Is she:

Sleepy?

Hungry?

Over stimulated?

Once a pattern is detected, practice prevention.

If each time you take your daughter to the mall, she ends up biting you, then the mall is probably too stimulating for her. Shop without her.

A teacher might notice a child bites right before naptime. Allowing the child to stay inside to help set out nap mats and be the first to lie down, might help her manage better.

SUPERVISION

The most basic prevention is supervision.

There is not always a detectable pattern to biting:

- Be available and responsive
- Comment on her activity at frequent intervals
- Make physical contact: hug; stroke her arm; rub circles over her shoulders

Supervision combined with the previous techniques can get most biting under reasonable control. Work with your child's caregivers to ease her through this difficult time.

One ten-year plus veteran director of a toddler program says that she has never had to ask a biter to leave. She credits this to teaching children how to recognize and respond to their emotions in appropriate ways; keeping demands for difficult behaviors such as sharing to a minimum; and watching for pre-biting patterns and practicing prevention.

A really persistent biter may need to become a teacher's shadow: as a helper, by sitting in the teacher's lap at group time, or by working alongside the teacher throughout the day. If the biting is excessive, a low adult:child ratio, (1:5 or less for toddlers), may be needed, which could necessitate a move to a smaller setting — at least in the short term.

PRE-TALK

Once children learn to speak, most biting incidents stop. For this reason, effective early communication may prevent or reduce biting. Proponents of sign language claim that by giving babies and toddlers the means to communicate their needs without words, frustration, and thus biting, will be lessened. (See *Sign with Your Baby* [Garcia, Northlight Communications, (877) 744-6263 or visit www.sign2me.com].)

AFTER THE BITE

In spite of our efforts, biting might still continue. If the biting is related to development, only time will fully resolve it. Try to focus on improvement (less biting) rather than perfection (no biting). When we understand biting from a young child's perspective, responding with compassion makes sense. Prevention, patience, and vigilance are the best tools we have through this difficult time. (For more on biting read *Positive Discipline: The First Three Years* [Nelsen, Erwin, & Duffy, Random House 2007].)

TRIPLE 'S' BITING RESPONSE

STOP!
Provide damage control.

STATE!
"No biting."

SOOTHE!
Address the needs of both children.

Teaching: When and How to Do It

Situation: What? When? How?

Last week, during her Friday afternoon visit with me, my granddaughter Mandy spilled her orange juice. She found this fascinating and discovered that she could fingerpaint the floor using this providential juice puddle. My first instinct was to yell out, "No. No. Stop!" But I now am blessed with the heart and mind of a grandmother, which makes anything Mandy does seem 'perfect' — or nearly so.

I stopped my outcry, focused on the side-to-side swipe of her adorable little orange juice-drenched hands, and realized that what I was seeing was the exact same movement needed to wipe up a spill. I grabbed some paper towels and placed them in her hands. Mandy stopped sloshing long enough to get a good grip on the towels and then went back to her floor polishing, now transformed into cleaning up the spill. We both grinned, delighted at our cleverness.

Solution

At age two, Mandy has lots of skills to learn. Wiping up spills comes along early because the opportunities are abundant, but we are all learning, all of the time. Whether learning new skills or teaching those skills, there are basic steps involved in each process.

TEACHING 'SKILLS'

Most skills are a series of smaller skills. There are also many types of skills: life skills, social skills, and emotional skills; each presents a unique teaching challenge:

• Life Skills

Life skills are easy to identify. Mandy is learning to wipe up spills. The puddles of milk and juice are easy to spot.

Life skills are those needed for day-to-day living.

• Social Skills

Social skills present a different challenge because there are so many possible applications. 'Mine', 'his or yours', and 'ours' are separate concepts that contribute to the bigger social skills of sharing, cooperation, and consideration.

• Mine, His, and Ours

In Chicago, when four-year-old Angela carries her special teddy bear from room to room and into bed at night, that teddy is 'hers'. 'Her' teddy provides a point of reference, helping her to understand that the bunny her brother Matthew sleeps with is 'his'. Each child learns 'mine' as part of the process leading to sharing. In New Zealand, Huhana, a Maori child who is also four years old, learns a different lesson. She is given the last serving of pudding and then told that she may not have it all to herself. She must share it with others. Huhana's culture places a higher value on the collective needs of the group. 'Mine' is not a concept that is supported in Maori culture, so sharing is taught in a different way there. Huhana learns the social skill of sharing as a reflection of her role within a larger community.

• Emotional Skills

Emotional skills can be quite complex. At age four, feeling angry with a playmate for not sitting beside him at preschool, Saul scowls and says, "You can't come to my birthday party" — an event at least five months away. The feeling is there, but words to express that feeling are not. Saul, as a Canadian child and a member of a Western culture that will expect him to express his feelings using words, will need to become skilled at doing so.

TEACHING 'SKILLS'

Pretty complex, isn't it? Whatever the skill — Angela's understanding 'mine'; Huhana's learning to respond to the needs of other group members; or Saul's ability to express his feelings with words — the teaching process will follow similar steps:

- Identify the skill
- Break it into parts
- Expect the possible

• Identify the skill

Sharing is a social skill. We can identify the skill, but remember that how and what we teach about sharing will produce different results. Huhana needs to learn to define herself in relation to other people. Setting up a situation where she is expected to do so, values sharing and community; meanwhile, Angela and her brother are learning to value and respect individual property and personal ownership.

I want to encourage my granddaughter Mandy's **independence**, another social skill. Teaching her how to wipe up after herself fosters the development of independence.

• Break it into parts

Mandy's feelings of competence and independence will not happen as the result of sopping up orange juice with a paper towel one time, but as the cumulative result of mastering many small steps. In Mandy's case, being able to clench the paper towels and coordinate her movements so that the towels and spilled juice meet up with one another are necessary preliminary skills.

Huhana will experience her connection to others through much more than the expectation of sharing a single serving of pudding.

• Expect the possible

What we teach is influenced by a child's ability level. I did not fill a bucket and try to teach Mandy to scrub my kitchen floor. If I had I would probably have had a bucket of sudsy water to mop up as well as orange juice or she might even have decided to climb into the bucket and splash about.

For both teacher and learner to achieve success, we need to expect the possible.

'TEACHING' SKILLS: FOUR STEPS

Once you know what you want to teach, the teaching steps are the same for any new skill. They are:

- *"Show me!"* Demonstrate/model
- *"Help me!"* Work together
- *"Support me!"* Coach/consult
- *"Hooray for us!"* Celebrate success

First: Show me — Demonstrate/model

What is it you want to teach? Children love to do what we do.

Imitation is the foundation of learning.

Life Skills

Mandy has watched me wipe up spills many times. As her coordination develops, I will teach her how to squeeze out a sponge and later how to use a mop that has been cut down to her size, always starting by modeling these actions.

Social Skills

Margaret, a teacher at Angela's preschool, sits down with a container of crayons for Angela and another child to share with her. Margaret places the crayons in the middle of the table. When Margaret finishes with the purple crayon, she replaces it in the container. When she sees Angela finish with the red crayon, she guides her to return it to the box. This continues with each crayon they use as Angela learns to share in a new way.

Emotional Skills

What is the first step of teaching children how to handle anger? What does your child see? The next time Saul's dad gets steaming mad, he announces that he is angry and needs to cool off, then heads to his room. Saul hears the emotion named **anger**, and observes an acceptable way to handle it.

Second: Help me — Work together
The second step of teaching a skill is to do it together.

Life Skills
When Mandy is a bit older, I will place small sponges where she can reach them. When she spills, I can say, "We need to get a sponge to clean this up," then do so together.

Social Skills
Angela's teacher passes a tray inviting children to share their lunches with a child who has forgotten his, thus giving Angela and her classmates an additional way to practice sharing.

Emotional Skills
While reading a story about an angry troll Saul's aunt says, "I see someone who is very mad. Do you?"

"The troll is mad," says Saul, nodding his head.

"Do you think that troll needs to calm down? Should he go to his room and cool off?"

"He needs to cool off," says Saul.

With his Aunt's prompting, Saul deepens his understanding of concepts he is learning (identifying **anger** and how to handle it) by applying them in a different situation.

Third: Support me — Coach/consult
The next steps in teaching a new skill involve being nearby: to offer support and encouragement; provide coaching; and supply tips, as needed or when asked.

Life Skills

Mandy spills and we both say, "Uh-oh!" This time I ask her what she needs to do about the spill. I do not tell her what needs to be done because this stage of learning gives Mandy the chance to practice the skill and experience her own competence, both of which support her growing independence.

Giving children an opportunity to demonstrate skill mastery is crucial to the development of self-esteem.

Social Skills

Angela's mom could suggest Angela look around her bedroom and decide if there were any toys she wasn't ready to share with her cousins before they came to visit. Then she might help Angela store the dolls she doesn't want to share in her closet the day the cousins were coming over. The choice of deciding to share strengthens the lessons Angela has been learning.

An adult in the Maori community might get Huhana's attention, hand her a basket of rhythm sticks, and smile encouragement, waiting for her to offer them to the other children.

Coaching supports success.

Emotional Skills

Saul, learning to use words to handle his anger, might tell Archie, "I was still playing with that truck. You took it! I'm mad." This statement allows Saul to express his anger and to learn to be assertive, both skills valued by his society.

THE ROLE OF MISTAKES

Remember learning to swim? Did you swallow water or get it in your eyes and nose? We can't make learning free of difficulty. Mandy will spill; Angela may grab a book from her friend's hands; and at times Saul will yell; or Huhana may ignore her brother.

*Just like swallowing water while learning to swim —
all learning includes mistakes.*

ENCOURAGEMENT

We need encouragement as we struggle through our mistakes. What encouraged you to get back into the water? Did a favorite uncle tell you about how hard it was for him to learn to swim as a kid, giving you the courage to climb back in again? When you managed to curl into a ball and float like a jellyfish, was your grandpa there to help you out of the water and say, "I knew you could do it!"

When Mandy uses a sponge to wipe up milk only to squeeze the sponge and recreate the puddle a moment later, I am there to tell her what a fine job she did using the sponge. I am also there to slide a bowl into position to receive the next sponge full of milk.

Mistakes are part of the process. Encouragement keeps us trying.

FINAL STEP: HOORAY FOR US! CELEBRATE SUCCESS

At last we come to the day of pride for both teacher and learner: successful mastery.

Life Skills

Mandy knows where the sponge is kept and how to use it. She sees herself as capable of doing things on her own.

Social Skills

Angela offers her new doll to a playmate. She understands sharing and initiates it. Huhana sees that her little sister has a taste of the cake served with tea and feels a strong connection to the others in her community. She has learned to take notice of the needs of others and see through her culture's **collective** perspective.

Emotional Skills

Saul says, "I'm angry! I need a cool off," and marches off to his room on his own. He has learned to name and handle anger, giving him a sense of empowerment.

NOW YOU

What skill do you want to teach? What skill is needed?

Model the skill; do it together; offer support.

That day of mastery will arrive.

"Hooray!" She did it!"

And so did you!

TEACHING 'SKILLS'

Identify the skill.

Break it into parts.

Expect the possible.

'TEACHING' SKILLS

"Show me!"

Demonstrate/model

"Help me!"

Work together

"Support me!"

Coach/consult

"Hooray for us!"

Celebrate success

#10

Bad Language

Problem #10 is about words,
in particular those defined as:
POTTY TALK and NAME-CALLING.
As children discover language, they learn the
power of words. It doesn't take long for them
*to discover the impact of a well-placed **bad word**,*
but there is also an aspect of humor to this
early word use. If you want to hear children chuckle,
just mention farts, poop, or booties.

From Potty Talk to Swearing to Name-Calling — Humor or Hurtful?

Situation: From a Child's Perspective

"At first all I had to do was coo, gurgle, or cry and I got fed, changed, or held. Then my coos changed into Mama, or Dada, or Gamma and something great happened. My sounds had magical powers. When my Mamas and Dadas turned into NOs, I wondered if words could get any better? Well, as a matter of fact — YES!

"It wasn't long after my 'NO' period had begun that people started paying attention to what came out of my other end. When I left a little something in the potty one morning, magic seemed to be pouring out of me — from both ends!

"But now I've discovered even better magic! Watch what happens when I say 'POOPY'!" Note: At this point our narration must end for our protagonist is convulsing on the floor in a fit of giggles.

Solution: Potty Humor

Sounds and the words they form usher in a true magical kingdom for children. Words hold power and the world reacts — sometimes in spectacular fashion. One mom said, "If you want to make my Abdu happy, just say 'butt'." Children love potty words. To them these words are high (or maybe, low) humor. They shriek with laughter at the word 'poop' and giggle with delight over, 'pee'.

Fascinated with her own body functions, a child's emerging vocabulary soon combines toilet training with the delightful shock value of potty words, to produce the hilarious plop of a gleefully uttered 'poopy'. When we give this language minimal attention (no matter how hard it is not to titter at their cuteness), it will keep early potty talk from becoming a bigger problem.

FARTS ARE FUNNY

Children find joy everywhere and as they become aware of other people's body functions as well as their own, it isn't long before they discover the joy of 'farts'. Now here is a word with a triple whammy. The actual action creates a wonderful sound, it is a source of embarrassment to everyone, and it is a 'naughty' word. For a child enthralled by the magic and power of words — winning the lottery couldn't compare to this thrill.

One approach is to make unacceptable words less potent through deliberate overuse. In the book *Walter the Farting Dog*, this awful and delightful word is mentioned on almost every page. After awhile, the shock value wears off and turns the word into a more ho-hum experience (but please note that **after a while** caveat).

THE ECHO EFFECT

A child's early language practice can also produce some mortifying moments for adults. A rueful mom tells the story of sitting in a doctor's waiting room. The room was quiet so that when her toddler dropped his toy and muttered, "Oh sh_ t," it rang out loud and clear. This mom knew at once that she had just heard her own voice echoed from her son's mouth, and realized it was time to clean up her language.

Children are great mimics and the **mirror neurons** firing in their brains prime them to reproduce what they experience. They don't invent words like the 'F-word'. They must first hear them. This second source of inappropriate language comes from playmates, the media, and friends; but it also comes, perhaps more often than we want to admit, from us.

The way these words get used — as angry epithets, to wound or belittle, and to bully are also testaments to the way children hear them used. If we want to eliminate such language (and behavior), the best place to start is with ourselves. Nonetheless, there may still be times we'll regress, needing to acknowledge and apologize for our language.

Even if such language does not offend you, you will be doing your child a disservice by not letting him know that some words are offensive to others. He will eventually be around people outside of his family and his ability to communicate in ways that are acceptable is going to matter. Children need to know the expectations of the society in which they live — and, yes, words CAN hurt.

When you and your child hear others use foul language, talk about it. Ask her what she thinks about those words. If she says, "It isn't nice to call names," or "mean words hurt people's feelings," she will better internalize these rules. Another response to offensive language is to send a child (or ourselves) into the bathroom to use them. It's boring to talk to yourself and without an audience the shock value disappears.

WORD 'KA-POW'ER
Language has power and certain words have definite 'KA-POW'er. Name-calling moves language to a deliberate and hurtful level. The meaning of a word matters less than the result it produces. Calling a playmate a 'dummy' gives the name-caller a sense of power, especially when the other child slinks away, gives in during a dispute, or quits competing for a coveted swing seat.

At one preschool the teachers were surprised to discover that the children didn't know what 'dummy' meant, even though some had used it to intimidate a class-mate, and the classmate had fully understood its hurtful intent. The bottomline is that hurting others cannot be allowed.

POSITIVE POWER

Name-calling turns language into something hurtful and is often a sign of inadequate skills or a symptom of feelings of powerlessness. We know that we need to teach social skills: to share, ask for what they need, or how to wait for turns. But children also need to experience appropriate power. This can occur through contributing behavior: handing out art supplies at preschool, helping plan a menu at home, or being put in charge of selecting the soup or crackers while grocery shopping. These diminish the need to seek power in hurtful ways.

The child being hurt by name-calling also needs skills, in particular self-assertive-ness. Adults can prompt this child to say, "Don't call me that name." Or, "It hurts when you call me that. Please stop now!"

The point is that we need to address many aspects of the problems symptomized by hurtful language, rather than focus on words alone.

FEELINGS NEED WORDS

Children also need to be able to name and express their emotions. A good rule of thumb is that children who use hurtful language (and this includes potty or swear words used in anger as well as name-calling) are often upset or feeling hurt. Marianna doesn't like it when Daddy won't let her watch television or play longer at the park. She can't name her feelings so she uses what she does know. She knows that potty words are naughty and that saying things in a loud voice gets attention (remember all that practice shouting "NO"?). So she combines these techniques and hollers: "You're a 'POOPY-BUTT'." Now that gets Dad's attention! Much early name-calling is a variation of potty talk, but its purpose turns to expressing strong emotions such as anger, disappointment, or frustration rather than that of humor. Thus, it requires a different response. First we make the boundary of acceptable behavior clear:

"It is not okay to call others names."
"Name-calling hurts others."
"You need to use my name when you speak to me."

We state the expectations and if a behavior continues we ask the child to leave the room (or the adult can step into another room) until the child is ready to use kind words. Doing this with a minimum of fuss and attention, but with calm consistency, will drain name-calling of its magic potential.

Next we add the skill. Spend time exploring what was going on and identify and name emotions:

"You felt disappointed that we had to leave the park. You wanted to play longer."
"You were angry when Daddy turned the television off and said it was bedtime. We can say how we feel without name-calling."

Suggest that next time she try saying, "Daddy, I really want to play longer," or "I'm MAD!" (here a loud voice may be acceptable, though the name-calling was not.) Children need to know that it is fine to say how they feel, even when those feelings are unpleasant, but it is not okay to call names or use words to hurt others.

We can acknowledge and commiserate with feelings, even if the need to leave the playground or go to bed remains the same:

"You really would like to play longer."
"You don't want to go to bed yet."
"You're upset because you want to watch your program."

We then follow these with a hopeful or encouraging statement:
"Maybe we can come back to the park this weekend."
"Let's record the rest of the program so you can watch it tomorrow."
Or, "Let's plan on watching a program together on Saturday. Which show should we choose?"

This last possibility helps to distract a child from the present upset and gives her something to look forward to, as well as experiencing a positive contribution through the planning process.

THE MAGIC CONTINUES

Words offer powerful magic. Children need to learn to use them in ways that are appropriate. Many of the issues with potty language, name-calling, and other **bad** language will appear and disappear within short developmental timeframes. We can extend those timeframes by overreacting and giving them too much attention. We can minimize them by setting firm boundaries, being consistent, and teaching skills that guide children towards acceptable behavior, as well as how to name and express their emotions. And it probably won't do any harm to laugh over the occasional fart — after all, farts can be funny — just ask any preschooler.

Children need to know the expectations of the society in which they live — and, yes, words CAN hurt.

Meaning:
It Isn't All in the Words!

Situation: What is Said

"I had it first!"
"You can't come to my birthday party!"
"You're always a meanie!"

Most of us respond to these statements in a predictable and seemingly logical way. "I had it first!" compels us to believe that it is our job to figure out who had what 'first', or whose rights may have been violated, but we all know that this is a thankless task, at best. Pronouncements of birthday party banishment may tempt us to point out that the next birthday is seven months away, but the reality of the date could not be less relevant.

As to the "You're always a meanie!" comment, well — most of us overstate things at times, don't we? The truth is that what children mean and what we understand or think they mean are often planets apart.

Solution: What Children Say, What They Mean

"I had it first" is pretty basic code for "I want it," and it is probably safe to add "I want it — now!" Who had what 'first' is really an adult issue.

"I had it first," is also an excellent means to get an adult to take sides, which then translates into "she loves me (or him) best!". Yikes! What does anybody really mean?

CODED FEELINGS

Moving on to the "You can't come to my birthday party"* statement, what we really have is a child saying "I'm mad." "My feelings are hurt"; "I feel upset with this other person," or even "You won't give me my way!"

Are we talking about that distant birthday? Not by a long shot! This young person can't say 'how' he feels and probably does not know 'what' those feelings are, either. Helping a child to recognize and name feelings is the basic need here:

"You really wanted to go to the park. You feel disappointed and upset. It is fine to say, 'I'm mad' when you feel that way. We all get mad at times."

"I MEAN NOW!"

"You're always a meanie!" Do you think you really are a terminal ogre? (Well, maybe some of us are, but there is a small chance that even the worst of us has a nice moment or two.) More likely what this child is saying is that she does not like what is happening 'right now!'

Children live in the present moment. Trying to remind them of the time you took them to the zoo; read four extra bedtime stories; or bought pizza and popsicles for lunch on Saturday is beside the point. **Now** is what matters, and has little to do with **nice** or even with **you**.

DIFFERENT THINKING

Part of the problem is that our thinking processes differ. Dr. Diane Levin, a professor at Wheelock College in Boston, Massachusetts, explains that children think in a series of **slides** rather than a flowing movie. A movie connects 'cause and effect', or 'input and outcomes', but individual **slides** don't do this. This is how it works:

A child sees a ball.
She wants the ball.
Someone else has the ball.
She takes the ball.
A tug-of-war begins.
She gets pushed down.

These events do not flow together as if they are connected to one another; each is a separate unit; a different slide image. With this kind of thinking, getting pushed down comes as a shocking surprise — every time!

We can help a child move from these separate slides to a flowing **movie** by helping her to see connections:

"You want to play with the ball. Your friend has the ball. When you grabbed the ball, what happened?"
"He pushed me."
"That's right. We need to figure out a safe way for both of you to play with the ball. What are some ways you can ask to use the ball?"
"Say please." "Ask, can I play?" "Give him another ball."
"Those are great ideas."

THE 'NO' WORD

There is one more word that needs to be mentioned. That is "No". The word "No" is quite magical if one happens to be two-years-old or younger. A toddler's "No" can be a simple reflex action; a new word that pops up without meaning. "Would you like some ice cream?" "No," she says, while nodding her head, and reaching for the dish of chocolate-studded creamy mint.

On the other hand, if everything is met with "NO!", maybe she is telling us that she is grumpy and wants to be left alone, or might need a hug right now:

"It's bath time."
"NO!"

"Do you want me to read a story to you?
"NO!"
"Would you like some apple juice?"
"NO!"

This type of "No", may also be a way to experience some power, "Look at me! I can control something in my life."

At times like this, be consoled that the ability to say "No," is really a good thing, especially in the teen years when she may be tempted to try drugs; ride with someone who has been drinking; or any of the many times we hope she will be saying "No".

CHILD 'SPEAK'

Child says:	Child means:
"I had it first!"	"I want it — NOW!"
"That's not fair!"	"I want it." (or to do it)
"I hate you!"	"I'm angry."
"You're a meanie." (or other term)	"I'm mad at you. I want my way."
"You can't come to my birthday."	"I'm mad." (disappointed, frustrated)
"No."	"I can stop or start the action. Wow! I (and my words) have power."
"You never . . ."	"At least not NOW (which is all that really matters)."

ADULT-ESE

Adult says:	Adult means:	Child hears:
"Maybe later . . ."	"I hope she will forget about this."	"You promised!"
"We'll see . . ."	"I hope she will forget about this."	"You said 'yes'."
"Another time . . ."	"I hope she will forget about this."	"Why not NOW?"
"No!"	"Stop! Don't do that."	"Wow! She noticed."

WHAT DO WE MEAN?

Let's look at the flip side of this situation, or what adults say, the meaning of which can be just as mystifying. When I offered to **draw** my granddaughter's bath water, not too surprisingly, she followed me into the bathroom and wanted to know where the crayons were. "Huh? Oh sweetie, I didn't mean that kind of **draw**."

Aside from 'drawing baths', with or without crayons, children are trying to make sense of what they see and experience. To say there is a communication challenge is to understate things.

WHAT DO WE MEAN?

"You need to listen."
"Act polite."
"Be nice to your little brother."

Listen is basic adult-ese for "Do what I tell you to do." Most children do in fact **listen**, but they often fail to **do** what they are told to do.

Be polite or **nice** and other such phrases leave a lot of room for individual interpretation. **Polite** behaviors comprise a lot of skills. **Polite** will not mean the same set of skills when sitting down to eat hamburgers in Grandma's backyard as those needed when attending Grandma's Nobel Peace Prize banquet.

What about **nice**? How would **nice** look right after little brother pulls his sister's hair? How can sister be **nice** while rescuing her favorite doll from little brother's mouth? In both of these cases, "Use gentle touches," might have given more useful guidance (and likely save little brother from sister's wrath or older sister from a session in time out).

MEANING MATTERS
From simple to complex there are plenty of opportunities to misunderstand one another. We can prevent a lot of conflict by making an effort to get the meaning right, since our words too often aren't up to the job on their own.

*For more on this topic, read "You Can't Make 'Em Do It" in *Positive Discipline for Preschoolers* (Nelsen, Erwin, & Duffy, Rocklin, CA: Random House, 2007).

More Problems

*We have made it through
The Top Ten Preschool Parenting Problems,
but there are MORE PROBLEMS that emerge
in these early years.
And problems aren't limited to children.*

*Some of the questions that come up for us are these:
What about me? • What about us?
What about our family? • How can I handle this?
What parenting tools are best?*

*In this final section we will look at:
Adult Issues
Family Issues
Hard Topics
Universal Tools*

Adult Issues

Many problems are unique to adults and their relationships.
What problems do adults struggle with the most?
My experience rates these as the top problems for adults:
intimacy, personal time, disagreements over parenting,
and parenting survival if relationships end.

In this section we'll cover:

What About Sex?
Time for Me: Kindling
When Parents Clash
Different Houses — One Child

What About Sex?

Situation: What About Sex?

"But what about sex?" a brave mother seated at the side of the room blurted out. The silence spread thicker than peanut butter. What had been an ordinary evening parenting class with discussions about toileting, sibling hassles, or getting ready in the morning became something quite a bit more interesting.

Gathering her courage and taking a deep breath, our valiant mom continued. "I mean when do you do it? When do you find time?"

There was a grateful sigh as the other parents nodded in agreement. Our heroine soldiered on. She released her hands from their death grip, combed her fingers outward through the noiseless air and mustered a final comment. "I mean we fall asleep when he does and he wakes up before we do. We are too tired to stay awake after we finally get him to sleep."

Heads were nodding vigorously around the room by this time. Then everyone began to talk.

Solution

Your life as a couple may have begun with shared adventures, stargazing into each other's eyes, and a romantic flutter or two. Somewhere between those early days and these late nights pacing with Junior there must have been some additional flutters as well. Full time job pressures; on-demand feeding schedules; and teething tots quickly drain away most of that romantic pizzazz. But everyone still needs it!

When couples let the intimate part of their relationship lapse, the joys of parenthood will not make up for it. And when the relationship that started this family unit is in trouble, the child(ren) are in trouble, too.

Remember how creative you were back in the days when you weren't supposed to be having sex? A few of you probably managed to outwit your parents, chaperones, and the occasional drive-in attendant. Now you face a new challenge. This time the people you have to outwit, sneak around, and generally befuddle are not your parents — but your kids!

There was a magazine article that appeared a few years ago. The title was something like "Mama's Nightgown's Inside Out." It was written as a memory piece. The author and her siblings noticed that on the mornings that mama and papa appeared at breakfast and mama had her nightgown on inside out, there was a definite *joy de vivré* emanating from the folks. "Mama's nightgown's inside out" signaled that the day was off to a good start, and it wasn't until they had their own kids that it occurred to them just what made mama and papa so cheerful and how mama might have come to get her nightgown on wrong.

GET CREATIVE

Use your creativity to inject a bit of procreativity back into your lives. Forget the bed or a cozy evening snuggle. Claim your home in the daylight. Take the little ones to child care, grandma's, or the neighbor's for a few hours and sneak back home to enjoy a little childfree lack of inhibition. Don't think just in terms of a little action in the dead of night. If your bathroom door locks, try a quickie (-er), shower and remember that baby's naptime can be used for more than stoking the washing machine. Recognize opportunity when it snoozes right on your doorstep.

Make what happens between the two of you at least as important as getting to the supermarket in time to stock up on disposable diapers before your coupon expires.

In and out of that fateful parenting class 'sex after kids' proved a lively topic. One parent said, "Thank goodness for Saturday morning cartoons." (This is another incentive for teaching your children how to serve their own cereal.) Of course, be sure children are safe and within earshot.

"The piano saved us!" claimed another parent. Her husband took up piano. At bedtime he played soothing lullabies and the little ones nodded right off to sleep, leaving the big ones awake — and alone!

PROTECT PRIVACY

A bedroom with a locking device is pretty essential if parents want to have anything approaching a private life that includes sex. Nothing turns hot and heavy to limp and frustrated faster than a two-foot high person climbing up onto the bed for a snuggle, requesting a glass of water, or telling you that his sister just called him a name. (You could think of a few names yourself at such moments!)

A telephone answering machine helps, too, so that Granny does not need to trade recipes at your life's more luscious moments. The point is that it is okay to stay secluded now and again. Just remember — you are doing it for the kids!

When couples let the intimate part of their relationship lapse, the joys of parenthood will not make up for it.

THINK VARIETY

Of course, sex and intimacy need not be joined at the hip. Try buying some foot care products and give each other pedicures. Even if massaging pinkies doesn't lead to other kinds of friction, the sensations are heavenly all on their own. Neck rubs, hand massages, and scalp caresses can create their own measure of bliss.

STAY AWAKE

• *Plan ahead*

Try drinking that espresso in the late afternoon or evening to keep you going longer than the kids.

• *Take your own nap*

A few Zs in the middle of the day just might help you keep your eyes open at day's end. After all, which matters more — folding those sheets or what happens under them.

• *Build in opportunity*

One couple took up yoga. After the children were asleep, they closed their bedroom door, folded themselves into human pretzels, and began deep breathing. Whenever one of them decided to do an *asana* or two without benefit of clothes, the postures got more interesting and the breathing heavier.

SINGLE PARENTS

Certainly not every child is born into a world of two parents, 2.5 children, and a family dog. Still, all adults need companionship, even those raising children on their own. The challenge for single parents is to be both single — and parents. Carve out time for a social life that does not include your children. Some extra cautions apply. Try not to expose children to every new person to enter your life. When children become attached to another adult, they will feel the loss of that person from their lives if the connection ends. Waiting until a relationship develops a degree of real commitment protects children from repeated losses.

It may seem like an impossible juggling act, but keeping in mind that your needs are important removes the guilt ball from among those whizzing past your head.

JUST DO IT

Parenthood and sex can coexist. When sex lives are lively — everyone stays satisfied.

Remember — you're doing it for the kids!

Rekindling Our Inner Fire

Situation: Rekindling Our Inner Fire

At 2 a.m. your toddler begins to whimper, then howls. You grope your way to his bed, pick him up, change his diaper, and pat him as he relaxes back to sleep. But, it seems that no sooner do you crawl back under the covers and close your eyes, that the alarm blares its 6 a.m. wake-up summons.

Wresting the children out of pajamas, into their clothes, and through a hurried breakfast of cold toast (with nothing for you) is next. Child care drop off, though mercifully without drama, is followed by a slow crawl through freeway traffic, interspersed with sips of cold coffee from your Styrofoam® cup.

At work, a reprimand from your boss for an unfinished report; a soggy sandwich eaten while catching up on e-mail; and two aspirin gulped down to quell a raging headache make up the day.

Back at home, you discover that the only dinner ingredients available are a cardboard carton of macaroni and cheese (at least something the children will eat!) and some very limp carrots. You are still pushing around a mushy forkful of orange glop when your three year old races in, tears streaming down her cheeks, to tell you her brother just bit her — YOU HAVE HAD IT! You storm from your chair, order your sobbing daughter to her room, and plop your son in his crib, while yelling that "This kind of behavior has got to stop — RIGHT NOW!"

Solution: Whose Behavior?

Don't we have to wonder whose behavior is being referred to? We all have days like the one above and even the most patient among us will 'lose it' at times. But, though we may agree that being a parent can be stressful, few of us make our needs a priority — or even a consideration.

Imagine a campfire or fireplace with a prominently displayed stump of wood. In order for that stump to provide warmth, something has to happen. That something is called **kindling**. Those bits of paper, small twigs, and medium-sized branches that constitute **kindling** can transform a stump into welcoming warmth. Well, it isn't only wooden stumps that need kindling.

KINDLING

Each of us is very much like that unlit log — cold and lifeless with nothing to release our inner warmth, the warmth our family members seek from us, without kindling. What constitutes human kindling? Human kindling are those things that energize and encourage us. Here are some of the types of kindling I hear listed in my parenting classes:

- a warm bath or shower
- time to read
- time alone
- time with friends
- time to talk to friends
- exercise: yoga, swimming, running, gym workouts, bicycling
- playing music
- listening to music
- time for hobbies (though few even mention this one, as it seems so impossible)

Couples also have lists of what helps keep the flame of their relationships burning. These are some of their ideas:

- time together (away from family responsibilities)
- time with friends
- time for sex (and other types of shared intimacy)
- playing sports together

One thing both lists have in common is the mention of **time**. Another is that the need to re-kindle ourselves isn't OPTIONAL! That's right — meeting our own needs is every bit as necessary as providing food, rest, or shelter for our children.

Airlines remind us that, "In the event of an emergency, please place an oxygen mask on yourself, before your children." Why? The answer is simple: if we're unable to breathe, how can we help them? The same is true for meeting our other needs. All the discipline in creation won't be enough to make up for the loss of that loving warmth that only we can provide — warmth that doesn't get ignited on its own.

But how? When? There is no time! The answer to all of these is the same: NOT OPTIONAL. A half-dozen deep breaths might be the best we can manage. So, breathe. After all, if we don't find time and means to care for ourselves — who will?

FINDING TIME: THINK SMALL

Tammy, a nurse, began to use the stairs at the hospital to go to and from her breaks. Five floors down, five floors up — and on week two she realized she was no longer gasping like a dying locomotive by floor three. Another benefit was her improved focus, further reducing her daily stress.

We all know that exercise is valuable, but "Ya-da, ya-da, ya-da," right? We say we will join a gym, take part in a triathlon, start jogging . . . one of these days. Well, how small can you think? These are admirable goals, but they may be way TOO BIG. If we set goals that are TOO BIG, we end up feeling discouraged. So, think small. Think tiny. Think maybe only one flight of stairs instead of five, and who knows — once you have begun, adding another flight may not seem all that impossible.

FINDING TIME: PLAN AND PAY AHEAD

Another strategy is to 'plan and pay ahead'. Evan wanted to sign up for a series of weight-training classes at the gym near his office. They began at 6:30 a.m., but that would mean leaving an hour earlier for work. So he talked the plan over with his wife and they agreed that if he packed lunches the night before and gathered their twin sons' shoes, coats, and clothes for the next day, she would be willing to take over the morning routine.

Added to that was the fact that these classes had to be paid for in advance, so even if (or more likely, when) Evan didn't feel like crawling out of bed — the thought of that already spent money would prod him out the door.

'ANDS' NOT 'BUTS'

True, not everyone will have a willing partner around for support. This isn't a BUT, however, it is an AND. In other words, BUT you don't have someone to give you time to yourself, AND what will you do instead?

> *BUTS get bigger.*
> *ANDS get us going.*

"I want to exercise AND I could":

• Set up a babysitting trade with a neighbor or another child care parent.
• Find a gym with child care services and hours that work with my schedule.
• Ask Grandma or a neighbor to drop-off my little one at preschool to give me a half-hour for yoga.

Get the idea? NOT OPTIONAL.

FINDING TIME AWAY

Sherri and Sam could only manage a single day and night away from their home and children. They didn't want to spend this precious time mired in traffic, so they rented a room at a bed and breakfast ten minutes from their house. After a dinner out, they went to a nearby club and listened to a blues band. The next morning they slept in, made love, and read the paper over cups of coffee and warm croissants. By that evening they were laughing, holding hands, and ready to greet their children as the loving parents they wanted to be.

Single mom, Abby, was just as refreshed when she rejoined five-year-old Kyle after a weekend spent scrapbooking with two of her friends, while Kyle had been at his dad's. Instead of spending her time cleaning, catching up on laundry, and doing some reading — things she often did on Kyle's weekends away, what she had needed more was time with friends and a chance to use her creativity.

OTHER OPTIONS

What if there is no partner, money for a sitter, or ex-spouse in your picture? Once again, this is an AND — not a BUT. A half-day trade with another parent can give both a needed break, cost nothing, and pay out huge dividends for all. Single friends also love the chance to be an 'auntie' or 'big brother' for a day.

In extreme cases, when you are truly overwhelmed (and probably haven't paid attention to your own needs for awhile), many areas offer emergency respite care. Find these resources and use them. It is not shameful or selfish to do so. Your children will be cared for and you will get the break you need. Everyone will benefit.

FROM STUMP TO WARMTH

Kindling is prevention at its most basic. Our families need warmth — not cold stumps — and caring for ourselves is truly NOT OPTIONAL.

P.S.   If, by chance, you still think caring for you is selfish or optional, please look up my counseling number (or one in your area), as you may just be needing such a service sometime soon.

When Parents Clash

Situation: When Parents Clash

"I want my son to learn good table manners," says Margaret, "and I think it is important that he ask to be excused when he is done eating or request to have foods passed to him by saying, 'please pass the potatoes.' My husband, Mark, thinks such niceties are totally frivolous. He sees nothing wrong with Jeremy just getting up and leaving the table or reaching across to grab what he wants. It seems like Mark and I disagree on all kinds of things when it comes to parenting. I hate for everything to be a battle and I am worried that our son won't know who to listen to. Should I stand my ground on table manners?"

Solution

Standing your ground sounds like a military maneuver. Parenting is not a war. Instead of taking a stand like a noble Napoleon (who, if you remember, didn't fare so well), consider yourself part of a mega-merger. Two corporations, in this case you and Mark, have just merged and the two boards must now map out a new corporate structure.

When Mark was growing up, he and his brothers and sisters happily tucked into their French fries and played tug-of-war over the ketchup bottle. When any one of them reached the bursting point and could not suck down another limp morsel, he or she would waddle off into the next room. Life was lovely. Satisfied belches resonated throughout their happy home.

Meanwhile, you and your parents were curling pinky fingers as you murmured refined, "May I please have some more quiche" requests. After the dessert course you dabbed the crumbs from your lips and were granted permission to rise and part company with your devoted parents. The sounds of clinking crystal and classical music trailed behind you as you promenaded out of the dining hall.

Well, maybe Mark wasn't really wallowing quite that much or perhaps your pinky wasn't actually curled, but the worlds in which each of us grow up are every bit as varied. Not only are those worlds vastly different, but they are also, for each of us, the benchmark for **normal**. At three, or six, or even twelve, life as we know it consists of what happens within our own families.

It is a pretty safe bet that when Mark was rowing you down the river with moonlight painting stars in your eyes, neither of you thought to ask, "What is your attitude toward passing food at the dinner table?" Most of us don't. It is the entry of children into our lives that brings up such topics.

NEGOTIATION: THE 'POWER OF THREE'

When the differences between *Mark of Happy Hollow* and your own *Delicate Sensibilities Inc.* collide, try to figure out why. Arrange for the two of you to spend some time talking. Find out the **why** behind your attitudes. Get curious. Neither one of you is **right**. You each just have different versions of **normal**.

Adult life is seldom a mirror image of your own childhoods. The energy of this new family will grow and develop by applying creativity to craft a new **normal**. 'Mark's way' and 'Your way' must emerge as 'Our way.'

Let's revisit mealtime at *Mark and You Inc.* There are more options than either murmuring a request to be excused or rolling away from the trough. Start brainstorming. Come up with at least three ideas. The process of finding three alternatives gets us out of being stuck in our own corners, dug into our own positions, or feeling frustrated and helpless. Let's try this out. Here are three ideas:

• Say "Thank you" for the meal when finished.
• Say **something** before getting up to leave: "I'm full," "I think I'll get back to my homework," or "I'd like to finish the chapter on *Plato* before the nightly news comes on."
• Slap the table, click your heels, and shout "Well done!"

Please note that not every idea presented must be ideal. In fact, throwing in a few nutty ones relaxes the atmosphere. When we feel lighter and more playful, creative energy gets flowing, which usually leads to more productive results.

PRIORITIZE: CLOSING THE DEAL

There will be many opportunities to disagree over parenting. Everything from the proper use of the toothpaste cap, to chores and appropriate discipline will pop up for airing. Decide what matters most to you. If saying "Please" when asking to have food passed rates as number one on your list, then say how important it is to you and ask if the other person could live with your style. In return offer to live with something that really matters to him. This is how 'Our way' gets forged.

NO HOSTILE TAKEOVERS

It is unrealistic to think that parents can always present a united front. When (not if) disagreements do surface, don't worry. They aren't fatal.

A clash over whether to send Junior to his room or not does not mean that your marriage is about to dissolve. Finding out that there are things that you and your partner do not agree on when it comes to Junior is **normal**. Learning how to deal with the inevitable differences is the real challenge. Follow the three steps:

• listen
• negotiate
• prioritize

Sometimes things will happen just the way you want them to. Try not to smirk or look too self-satisfied. Other times something better will emerge. Just relax and enjoy this great new idea. And some of the time you will need to practice not wincing. Take some deep breaths and apply civility.

It (whatever **it** was this time) will matter less and begin to seem **normal** after awhile. Aim for a successful merger — rather than a hostile takeover.

THE 'NEW NORMAL' MEGA-MERGER

Listen: Be curious and respectful.

Negotiate: Discuss options. Be creative.

Prioritize: Practice 'give and take'. Be gracious.

Live happily (or at least more compatibly) ever after.

Separation and Divorce:
Different Houses — One Child

Situation: Different Houses, One Child

SCENARIO #1

When Tara comes back from visiting her dad, she turns up her nose at our dinner salads. At her dad's house she gets French fries, pizza, and potatoes chips whenever she wants them. Here, we eat at mealtimes and offer carrots or fruit for snacks. It is always a struggle to get things back in balance. Her dad refuses to respect the dietary choices I want for Tara.

SCENARIO #2

I signed my son Nathan up for the soccer team at our church. He loves playing on the team, but when games or practices fall on dates he is with his mom, she won't take him because she objects to some of the beliefs held by my church. I've told her the sports program has nothing to do with my church's theology, but she doesn't believe me. She is undermining the lesson of responsibility that I want Nathan to learn by being on a sports team.

SCENARIO #3

*My ex-spouse has begun taking away the **privilege** of playing with friends on the weekend if our son Elijah brings home a bad report from school that week. I think* *this is too harsh a punishment and am furious about it. Elijah only sees his dad on alternate weekends, but I dread them more and more.*

Solution

Tara, Nathan, and Elijah's parents are forgetting one important detail: they are no longer married to their child's other parent! If that other parent hadn't done so many things they disliked, they might still be a couple! The problem is that although the marriage ended, the relationship didn't.

Children tether the lives of their parents, stepparents, and extended families to one another. When warring parents continue to battle over **what**, or **how**, or **when** the other parent does things, children begin to feel like they are being jerked back and forth between those they love by an invisible bungee cord.

AIMING BLAME

It is tempting to blame a child's misbehavior on the other parent's 'too lax', 'too strict', or 'inappropriate' parenting, but in fact some of what we see as tantrums, talking back, or obstinacy could be expressions of frustration, anger, or sadness that a child cannot articulate.

Blame aims frustrations outward and if the target is an ex-spouse, it is a target that cannot be hit without everyone getting wounded.

RESPECT AND LETTING GO

One cannot control an ex-spouse's choices. Accept that. French fries at dad's and salads at mom's are the way it is — and the way it will continue to be. What is likely to cause more indigestion for your child is to feel that her loyalties are being measured in lettuce leaves or ketchup packets.

If children see **respect** they learn it. Tara's parents make different food choices. **Respect** means accepting rather than criticizing those differences (even when the differences are hard to swallow!).

At some point Nathan will be able to explain to his mom the commitment he feels to his sports team. Missing some games early in life won't make learning responsibility to a team impossible. What is more important for Nathan is not feeling that he is scoring points for either parent by his choices.

Elijah's mother's concern over his dad taking away privileges relates to discipline. Elijah's father's discipline may be distasteful, but if it does not pose a threat to Elijah's safety, his mother needs to refrain from undermining it. The message of respect matters more than the privileges that might be at stake.

PROTECTION

The exception to this premise is when a child's safety is at risk. Consider these two criteria:

- Is this person physically or emotionally abusive?
- Is this person a danger to a child's health or well-being?

If either answer is truly "yes", then seek legal protection for the child. If there is real danger — **actions, not words**, are needed.

BACK AND FORTH

Anticipate the need to readjust when moving from one household to another. Keep activities on the day a child arrives or returns slow-paced and familiar. Consider creating a special return ritual such as pizza at Piecora's or a bubble bath and spa night. Find time to be alone with your child and listen to him. Each of you needs to reconnect.

If your child acts out, be clear about your rules and expectations and stay kind. It is possible to be both.

"You seem angry tonight but it is still not okay for you to yell at me. We can talk when you are ready to speak in a quieter voice."

"I know that you are allowed to watch television later at your mother's, but here bedtime is 8:00 p.m. Even though it is disappointing, our rule stands."

AT HOME — NOT ADRIFT

Imagine going to visit friends or family members in another town and discovering that you forgot to pack your toothbrush, left behind a treasured necklace, or a suitcase gets lost. One father understood this experience better as it applied to his daughter Magda's weekly visits, after using an activity from the *Parent Report Card* (Duffy & Crary, Parenting Press, 1998). For item #5: *Provides me with my own space in our home*, Magda gave her dad a failing mark, a grade that got him to do some special homework.

Since her parent's divorce, Magda had been carrying her clothes back and forth in a plastic grocery bag whenever she went to her dad's new apartment. She slept on the sofa, had to remember to bring over her storybooks, and had no place to store extra jeans, socks, or her favorite dolls.

> *In neither parent's home should a child feel like a visitor,*
> *no matter how short the time spent there is.*

Children need to have their own space, clothes, and toys at both houses. The next week, Magda's dad purchased a used set of drawers, took Magda shopping for clothes and toiletries, and set out two baskets in the corner of the kitchen for her to store books, blocks, and dolls. Magda began to feel 'at home' in both her parents' houses.

Children journey every few days, once each week, or weeks or months at a time from one home to another. Adjusting can be tough. If both places **feel** like home, the transition between each will be smoother.

MANY WAYS

Children learn that it is fine to talk and make noise while watching a video in the family room at home, but not acceptable to do so at the movie theater. They learn to sit at a desk during math class and run around the field at recess. They know that Grandma allows them to chew gum and mom doesn't (and most are smart enough not to point this out to either Grandma or mom!).

In the same way, children will come to understand that mom's house and dad's house have different rules.

BUNDLED TOGETHER

There is an African word *Ubuntu* that Jason Carter explains in his book, *Power Lines* (National Geographic, 2002). *Ubuntu* translates as being "bound up with others in the bundle of life, for a person is only a person through other persons."

This concept of *Ubuntu* invites us to see each child as becoming who and what she is and will be, through her relationships with **all** the people in her life — including one's evil ex-spouse, new stepparents, or unfamiliar, as well as former, extended family members.

When parents accept both the limits and permanence of the relationship with their child's other parent, a child need not feel disloyal for loving both. Children thrive **because** of the adults who love them — not in spite of them.

Ubuntu is universal.

Family Issues

Children transform us into families.
Just what does that mean and how do we connect
*with one another within this new creation of **family**?*

A lot of family life revolves around how we spend time —
with one another (or not).
Next we take a look at:

Television
Hang Time
Time to Laugh
Traditions
Vacation

We Are What We Watch — Television and Screen Time

Situation

A little girl and her father sat in their living room watching as a man swallowed fiery torches on the television screen. A visiting friend worried that the three-year-old girl should not see something so dangerous. The dad said, "She's not really paying attention."

As they spoke the scene changed to two acrobats — one bent into an arch while the other climbed onto his stomach. At once the little girl bent backward and called out to the visitor, "Okay, now you climb on me!"

Children are paying attention.

Solution: Seeing is Believing

Children believe what they see because their brains are still developing. One adult friend remembers, at about age three, hearing a woman on television say, "Hello. I am so glad to be with you today." My friend, believing this total stranger could see her, ran from the room terrified. Children do not differentiate real from pretend until they are five or older, nor do they interpret what they see, as adults might. When two preschoolers were told to **shake** before beginning a game, meaning to hold and shake hands, instead they both began to wiggle and shake. Young children interpret things literally. Remember when television studios stopped airing the image of planes crashing into the World Trade Center Tower on September 11? For young children, every repeat of that sequence represented the same event taking place over and over again.

For youngsters — seeing is believing.

MEDIA REALITY

The Kaiser Family Foundation released a report in October 2003 documenting that children six and under engage in **screen time** (television, computers, and video games) an average of two hours daily. The American Academy of Pediatrics advises against children under two watching any television, and yet 68 percent or more of children in this age group do so.

What we will do with this information is uncertain, but it is clear that **screen time** plays a potent role in children's lives today.

SEEING AND DOING

Children imitate what they see. The good news is that parents reported that 78 percent of what was imitated from the media was positive, such as sharing or helping, but an alarming 36 percent was of aggressive behavior (Kaiser Report, item #8).

Our three-year-old would-be acrobat serves to remind us:

Children are paying attention,
therefore, so must we.

Media access is one area where adults wield important discretionary power.

ORAL TRADITIONS — WHOSE VALUES?

Culture and traditions are passed from generation to generation through music, dance, and stories. Oral story telling, the passing down of stories from tribal elders, is a time-honored tradition. These stories contain beliefs, values, and detail events that connect us to the past as they weave generations together.

With the advent of the printing press, books and the written word largely supplanted oral story-telling traditions. The pen became mightier than the sword for shaping and changing attitudes.

Screen time has become today's storytelling medium, often nudging books aside. By documenting this significant societal shift, the Kaiser Report verified a cultural watershed. Has media become our link from the past, to the present, to the future?

SO WHAT?
As screen time has increased, the age of those watching has decreased. So what?

If screen time increases — what decreases?

Are there attention span implications? Because media events take place in several second or minute intervals, will children be trained to have shorter attention spans? Does screen time replace exercise time? Will childhood obesity increase? What are the public health implications? What role will books continue to play? Will learning to read be affected? Will reading diminish in value? Questions outnumber answers.

A READING CULTURE
The Kaiser Report found that four- to six-year-old children, in households with **heavy** television viewing, were 'less likely' to be able to read, though it did not say that the one caused the other. The critical information was the documented relationship involving screen time, lowered reading ability, and diminished time devoted to daily reading (Kaiser Report: Items #4 and #6).

For books to remain valued, people must be able to read. Reading means being read to, viewing books as valued resources, and devoting time to reading practice.

NOT RIGHT OR WRONG, BUT AWARE

The Kaiser Report gave us important information, the implications of which society must evaluate.

Change brings challenges.

One stay-at-home mom commented that those most vocal against television and videos "aren't home with their kids all day." True. Entertaining and keeping track of young children is exhausting, and 45 percent of parents admitted to using videos and television to occupy their children (Kaiser Report: Item #15).

*Screen time is not a **right** or **wrong** issue, but it is an issue.*

We live in a media world — and so do our children. What we want is for that three-year-old girl watching someone swallow fiery torches to be more influenced by the dad whose lap she watches from, than by what she watches from his lap.

Can it be done? How can screen time be tamed without resorting to a prohibition-like lifestyle? The answer is: Pay attention.

CHOICES MATTER

Here are some steps to consider:

- Turn off the television when no one is watching. Doing this allows adults to be aware of what their children are exposed to.
- Do not place a television or a computer in a young child's bedroom. The same reason as above applies. This also makes it easier to enforce time and content limitations.
- Limit daily screen time. According to the Kaiser Report, when parents enforce their media rules, children are more likely to read daily and to spend more time playing outdoors (Kaiser Report: Item #9).
- Monitor programming for appropriateness. What best represents the cultural inheritance you wish to pass on: the stories and values of *Lilo and Stitch* or those of *South Park*? Choices matter.

- View programs together. When not choosing the programming, watching a program with a child gives an adult the opportunity to question, discuss, and help a child interpret what she sees.
- Choose non-commercial programs. Most videos from the library, such as animated versions of children's books, do not promote consumerism. Those profiting from a potential lunchbox purchase, collectible cartoon doll, or imprinted t-shirt are not likely to place your child's best interests at heart.
- Combine books and media use. Books on tape can bring media and the written word together, while still encouraging imagination.
- Read. Raise a reader. Read to your children. Read with your children. Model reading. Make time for reading.

Our choices matter.

"No, we won't do that acrobatic trick, dear.
Let's read a story, instead."

What About Time?
No Hang Time

Situation: No Hang Time

At noon in Seattle it is already 3:00 p.m. in New York and 9:00 a.m. the next day in Singapore or Australia, but for many children how their time gets filled does not change much from place to place.

In Singapore, children spend their days at school, their afternoons doing homework, and taking part in music, tutoring, or sports programs. On weekends they take science or calligraphy classes.

In Seattle and New York, children spend their days at school, their afternoons playing soccer or baseball, and doing homework. On weekends they join their teams for competitions, work on science projects, or sculpt bowls in pottery classes.

In Australia, children spend their days at school, their afternoons in sports or after-school programs, and their evenings doing homework. On weekends they play sports, watch sports, and maybe practice on their tubas or drums.

The affluent lives of many children often seem filled to bursting, but lacking one crucial commodity: 'hang time.'

Solution

Hang is American shorthand slang for **hanging out**. The meaning of **hang time** is not complex. **Hang time** is doing nothing — on purpose. It is a time to **hang** onto some part of the globe and just let it rotate with you aboard.

It seems that no matter where they tread on this globe, many children's feet don't ever stop moving, nor do their hands, fingers, or the rest of their body parts. There is just very little **hang time**, anywhere. Wherever technology promises to save us time and effort we humans seem obsessed with filling that time and **doing more**.

More defines lifestyles. Children must **do more**, **learn more**, and **have more**. For children to **have more**, adults must **earn more** and, therefore, **work more**, which means there is **less time** to be with these children to whom we are giving **more**.

More equals less time.

WHEW!

The less time, the more we try to cram into it. Parents get out the scheduling books, filling in pages with violin lessons, soccer practices, and math tutoring sessions for their children so that their children can **learn more**, which will help those children be able to **earn more** and, therefore, **be more** and **have more**.

Whew! Don't you get tired just reading about it? Add to that the common complaint parents hear when there is actually a moment in the hustle of a day left unfilled, "Mommy, I'm bored!"

Our children don't even know **how** to **hang**.

RECONNECTING

Is **hang time** important, worthwhile, and desirable? I remember a story that often comes back to me. I don't know the source or whether it actually happened, but the concept is worth sharing.

There was an explorer traveling in a remote part of the world. He had hired numerous natives of the region to transport his supplies. At one point, after an intense three-day trek, his helpers all sat down and stopped moving. He tried to get them to continue, but not a one budged. He paced and stomped and threw his hat down in exasperation and asked the head guide why the others refused to move. The guide looked at him and said, "We must rest here awhile."

"Whatever for?" said the man.

The speaker explained, "We must allow our spirits to catch-up with our bodies." It seems they had been moving so fast that their bodies had outpaced their spirits, leaving their spirits behind. The workers had stopped to allow their spirits to connect back up. And there they sat.

Isn't that a great image — that we somehow leave parts of our very souls scattered in disarray behind us when we move too quickly across this earth? When I travel I think of this story. Modern-day parlance for allowing our spirits and minds to catch up with our bodies might be what we refer to as **jet lag**. As I sit munching my portion of pretzels, I visualize a trail of little particles — my inner self — scurrying to keep pace with the speed of the plane. They get blown astray, left to search and scramble toward each other as they follow my body's jet-propelled progress.

No wonder we are tired when we stumble down a ramp upon arriving, hundreds or thousands of miles ahead of those myriad particles of ourselves.

LIFE LAG

It sometimes seems as if the lives of many children and parents are massive cases of **life lag**. Between the rush from classroom, to dance studio, to basketball court; the gulped-down morning muffin; sprint through the grocery store for milk; or the last-minute stop to replace a missing school notebook; our spirits get scattered like confetti, broadcast from doorstep, to car door, to school desk.

Is it time for you and your child to let your cells regroup? Maybe we can all learn from the wisdom of those weary natives. Days do not need to be stuffed like holiday turkeys; crammed to capacity like too-small suitcases; or filled until they overflow like clogged sinks. We all need **hang time**.

MEMORY-MAKERS

What is one of your early memories? Is it the extra spelling lesson you labored over in fifth grade or the hour you spent with Dad listening to cooling rain pelt the patio roof on a hot summer's evening?

Is it an additional day of soccer practice, one long-ago season, or licking the drips from an ice cream cone with your visiting Aunt Mary while sitting at the wobbly kitchen table?

Is it the clay coaster made at a weekend art class or kicking through piles of crunchy leaves with Grandpa, while walking his cocker spaniel, Ginger, through the alley behind their house?

Spelling, team sports, and art classes are all valuable but:

Hang time provides the memories our souls treasure.

LOOK AROUND

See if you can spy any loose bits of your spirit or your child's, drifting overhead. Then stop and sit together a moment. Notice the raindrops dotting a fence rail; the splashing sound of sparrows enjoying a puddle; or the tangy pine smells of a spring afternoon. Feel that invisible cloud form overhead as your spirit reconnects. Savor this moment of wholeness.

Squeeze in some **hang time** and fill your hearts with the treasure of time. You will truly **have more** of what matters most.

A Time to Laugh:
Childhood is Not Forever

Situation: Learning to Laugh

This morning Betty wanted to pull the quilt over her head and not get out of bed. The sink was full of last night's dishes; anyone passing near her daughter Jessica's high chair would need to unglue his feet from the floor; and she had a report to finish that was already two days late. When Betty heard Jessica's sleepers scuffling down the hall she groaned, then sighed and tossed aside the covers.

She found Jessica sitting in the middle of the hall, adding the finishing touches to the rosebud pink lipstick that spread from her cheeks to her chin. Betty started to laugh and cry at the same time, and then gathered Jessica into her arms for a big hug, getting her own robe smeared with a layer of rosy goo.

Jessica puckered up and kissed her mom back, transferring a generous portion of pink to Betty's nose. It was a moment Betty wouldn't exchange for an army of personal housekeepers, a picture-perfect kitchen, or a day of pampering at a spa. (Well, maybe the spa might tempt her — in a weak moment!)

Solution

Think back over the past day, week, or even month. How often have you laughed with your child? When did you last have fun together? There is such an abundance of things to bemoan, fuss over, and stew about; but there are probably far more things worth celebrating. Can you name one?

If you haven't noticed anything enjoyable of late, perhaps your lens on life is in need of some polishing.

MOMENT-TO-MOMENT

Raising a child is a moment-to-moment experience. One moment you are separating squabbling toddlers and the next you are called upon to soothe and console an innocent-eyed urchin with a splinter in her finger.

The washer breaks down with a full load of half-washed towels just as your little one shows up at the door clutching the head of a daisy saying, "For you, Mommy!"

You are 20 minutes late for work, but young Davie is still sitting on the potty seat, actually **doing** something there for once.

No doubt about it. Raising kids is a messy, frustrating, and joyous job. The three come all smeared together in one life-sized finger painting. We need to take the time to sort out one color from the other, while marveling at the magic of the whole creation. It is easy to see just a muddy smudge if we don't use our hearts as well as our eyes to see.

PERSPECTIVE

Here is a favorite story told to me by one mom. It occurred after a weeklong home-stay for her son's chickenpox. Margo was on the phone, trying to catch up on some office work, when she realized how quiet the house had been — never a good sign. She hurried into the bedroom to discover little Randy, sitting naked on his bed, covered with colorful felt pen lines, to which he was adding yet another flourish.

Instead of her first reaction (instant horror), an image flashed through Margo's mind of all the dot-to-dot coloring books they had gone through during this chickenpox-induced confinement. Margo took a deep breath (well, several) then began to chuckle. Randy had recognized that his whole body resembled a giant dot-to-dot picture, and was acting accordingly. She replaced the permanent marker in his hand with a washable one, and then joined him in connecting the rest of the dots.

Instead of this moment resulting in a spanking, scolding, or time-out, Margo and Randy shared an episode that will become a treasured family legacy. One day, far into the future, as Randy and his children gather around the dinner table, he and Grandma will tell and retell the story of his dot-to-dot chickenpox as they swap 'remember when' tales of his childhood. The laughter generated on that long ago day will echo far into the future.

MEMORIES

It is surprising the things we remember. The day I spent singing songs on the bridge with three carloads of preschoolers on a field trip comes to mind. Partway across the bridge the tailgate of a truck had come loose, sending its cargo of metal pipes cascading onto the roadway. The entire bridge passage was blocked with no way to turn around. I can't tell you where our field trip had been headed, but I remember singing several hundred rousing choruses of "Jingle Bells" that hot July day.

UNEXPECTED INSIGHTS

Sometimes an unexpected moment of discovery occurs. One tired dad arrived home with his preschooler and instead of the rush to prepare dinner, cope with his daughter's demands, and struggle through their usual routine, he flopped down into a rocking chair, too tired for anything else. His little girl crawled onto his lap, snuggled up, and they cuddled for about 20 minutes. She told dad about her child care's new sandbox and dad laughed as she described the teacher's dismay over the visit a neighbor's cat had made to this sandbox overnight.

Later, when he began to fix dinner, an often-cantankerous part of their day, things proceeded without a hitch. Those few moments of loving reconnection had transformed them both — and given dad insight into a better way to approach their evenings. From then on, hugs would come before food.

CHILDHOOD IS NOT FOREVER

Instead of all the things that aren't working, look for your own joyous moments today. Be sure your lens on life hasn't become too cloudy to see the everyday magic of these fast-paced and fleeting years.

Childhood is not forever,
even though it sometimes seems that way.

Memories Are Made of . . .
Traditions and Rituals:
Life's Defining Moments

Situation: Life's Defining Moments

As soon as I said we were going to make Easter cookies, my three year old began tugging the ironing board out of its closet. "What are you doing?" I asked. "Easter cookies," she said. We stared at one another a moment — and then I remembered.

Each year I make a special anise-flavored Easter cookie, the ones I learned to make as a child in Grandma's kitchen beside my mom and gathered aunts. Since we made these only once each year and there were a lot of us, we made a lot of them, which means that I, too, make A LOT!

Once these cookies are baked to golden perfection, we frost them in pinks, greens, and that muddy color you get when you try to make purple using food coloring. Oh yes, and lots of chocolate. Then the frosting must harden, or they would all stick together, which brings us back to the ironing board.

As a new family with one child and little money or furniture, the small table we had couldn't hold all of those drying cookies, so the previous year I had hauled out — you guessed it — the ironing board. Thus today, my daughter was tugging out our ironing board. A new tradition had been born.

Solution: Traditions and Rituals

According to the dictionary traditions are customs handed down from one generation to the next, with rituals being more formal acts. John R. Gillis, of the Emory Center for Myth and Ritual in American Life, describes rituals as links that erase time — at once bringing together generations, past and present — as well as those yet to be born. My Easter cookies were all of these.

SIDELINED CONNECTIONS

One of the least visible changes in modern Western culture is the disappearance of our everyday rituals. Under the sponsorship of the Alfred P. Sloan Foundation, six long-term projects were launched to examine the family fabric of Americans. Part of what they found was that many of our everyday connections are disappearing: the dinner table (less than one-third of families eat together more than two times per week); shared spaces at home (children have private bedrooms, adults have home offices, while kitchens often stand vacant except for the time needed to microwave ready-made foods); and even personal greetings (hugs, kisses, or acknowledgements of one another upon arrival or departure) are vanishing.

Traditions and rituals — big and small, formal or accidental, even seemingly silly — matter because they connect and define us. They create belonging. When we bypass everyday rituals, we risk losing our human connectedness.

Though traditions and rituals may bend, expand, and even be reshaped — their presence in our lives is vital.

LOOK AROUND

Some traditions or rituals are easy to identify such as the way a family holds hands before each meal, but others are less obvious.

One year we had Thanksgiving dinner at a friend's house: there were no biscuits; the cranberry sauce came from a can; and the sweet potatoes lacked marshmallows. Our children were so upset by these anomalies that the next day we had to prepare a second feast — with all the **proper** foods. Until then, none of us recognized the role of those foods to our family's definition of Thanksgiving, but their absence made them visible.

SURVIVAL

Crisis can also bring our need for rituals into sharper focus. Joining hands in a circle, lighting candles, or praying and singing together will bring instant solace and connection after the loss of a loved one, as we mourn a school's shooting victims, or when we face the devastation of a tsunami. This same comfort exists in everyday acts.

Climbing into bed for a morning snuggle, reading *Curious George* night after night, or making Saturday pancakes are personal rituals that serve as our experiential Braille, when children and adults must grope through dark, painful, or anxious times.

A child who moves between households after a divorce seeks out the family cat, checks on the location of her marking pens, or pours herself a glass of orange juice in her special "Lion King" glass upon arrival, time after time, even if her visits are months apart. These rituals reassure and reconnect her, representing important anchors in the shifting currents of her life.

A child adopted as a toddler may insist on sleeping with a blanket over his crib, replicating the cocoon he experienced in his orphanage life. This sleep ritual goes beyond comfort and when we honor it we can help him bridge his very different worlds.

CELEBRATIONS AND FOOD

Special foods and holiday celebrations are the obvious traditions and rituals found in every culture. My friend's Passover meal signaled spring to all her friends. A neighbor's Ramadan sunset gatherings and the mingled sounds of laughter and Middle Eastern music floating through the night have become familiar entries on our shared calendars of experience.

COMINGS AND GOINGS

Many of our most defined rituals and traditions mark transition times: marriages graduations, funerals. Daily versions of these are bedtime and leave-taking — all transitions from connection to separation. A special wave, signing "I love you," or sharing bedtime stories helps ease the distress of such daily experiences.

Greetings and wakings mark reconnection, the transition from separation back to connection. Perhaps yours begins with a morning hug, a hello kiss, or the fragrance of a shared cup of warm cocoa. Touch, affection, and shared moments help us to reconnect.

WHO WE ARE

Traditions and rituals create a family's unique identity. I make Easter cookies, setting up an ironing board on which to dry them, and somehow we are connected to those same cookies spread over my Grandmother's daisy-printed plastic tablecloth decades before.

My friend replaces her mother's chicken broth with a vegetarian version for her brother's serving of matzo ball soup, but it is still her mother's soup. In my neighbor's kitchen, some of the women wear head coverings and some do not, but all share in the task of shaping grape leaves into dolmas from the common family recipe.

The ribbons that weave us together may change color, texture, or shape — but they link and hold us together.

THE WHOLE, NOT ITS PARTS

As important as the recitation of the Passover story; whether the sweet potatoes are topped with marshmallows or not; and which bedtime story gets reread — it is the sharing of our stories that matters most. Stories hand down our traditions, create our histories, and interpret our life experiences.

"Remember the time we couldn't eat Thanksgiving dinner until bedtime, because mom didn't know about thawing the turkey ahead of time and it was still frozen at eight o'clock that night?"

As we laugh and remember, tell and retell our stories, we shape attitudes, share values, and connect. The frozen turkey story speaks of an ability to laugh at one's mistakes and models an underlying compassion for our human imperfections. A child, who at some future date, overlooks a test page and fails his exam, has that family turkey disaster nestled deep inside him, to provide the resilience needed to bounce back from failure, and experience his own human imperfection with compassion.

RESILIENCE

Such a connection may sound far-fetched, but the Emory Center for Myth and Ritual in American Life has found that children who share in family narratives, score higher on tests that measure self-esteem as well as the ability to see themselves as having control over their lives, which translate into resilience.

We cannot always make the world safe, just, or avoid even temporary goodbyes, but we can nurture that inner core of resilience, that cushioning which enables us to bounce back, up, or beyond the struggles of each day.

CAN YOU SEE THEM, YET?

What are the invisible rituals of your daily lives? Are they special rhymes, "Good night, sleep tight, don't let the bed bugs bite," recited at tuck-in time; the annual phone call an uncle makes to play "Happy Birthday" on his trumpet; or cups of milky tea sipped around the dinner table? Are your connections frayed? Missing? Disappearing?

CONNECT UP

Traditions and rituals strengthen families. Family stories, both what we share and how we interpret them, transmit values, satisfy our need for belonging, bring solace, and connect us to who we were, are, and will become. They provide resilience as we remember our yesterdays, embrace our todays, and find the courage to face unknown tomorrows.

Traveling With Children —
Planes, Trains, and "Are We There, Yet?"

Situation: Surviving and Enjoying the Family Vacation

SCENARIO #1

I'm taking my daughter, who is 3½, from Los Angeles to Boston to visit my parents. We will be in the air six hours, then three-and-a-half, with a four-hour stop-over between flights. Any travel tips?

SCENARIO #2

This summer we are driving from Tucson to Sacramento to see my brother. We'll be in the car for a day and a half each way. How can I keep my three and five year olds from debating over which square inch of the seat belongs to one or the other for several hundred miles?

Solution: Vacation Time – Three Big Words

Before any family travel, chant these three words daily:

Prevention! Prevention! Prevention!

The best way to prevent displaying one's parenting skills while wrestling a child into an air craft seatbelt, chasing offspring across runways, or pounding on the gas station bathroom door insisting that the child inside "Open up to let your sister use the toilet NOW!" is to never get into those situations.

THE RULES

What behavior is expected? This requires planning. Will seatbelts be needed? When? Explain about seatbelt lights, and the rules of air travel.

Can car seats be unbuckled to lay down for a nap? Why not? What will make sleeping in a car easier? Small pillows? Lap blankets? A seat to oneself?

If a seat alone is impossible, what are the rules for the non-sleeper? No poking, quiet voice, staying on one's side of the seat?

What about the rules in stores or rest stops? Is holding a parent's hand necessary? One mom told about stopping to buy a book for her child at an airport kiosk. While she was paying, her son decided to look in a store a few shops away. The airport police, complete with search dogs, got involved before mom and child were reunited. A good rule: NEVER leave an area without a parent.

Spell out needed rules — before they are needed.

In another airport restroom I overheard a little girl tell her sister that she had to wait in the same stall with her until she finished, "so the bad mommies don't get you." This child had been given safety guidelines and was following them.

Children who know what to expect and what is expected;
make smarter and safer choices.

SLEEPING AND SOOTHERS

Another key to prevention is that of thinking through the basics: sleeping, eating, and toileting. No matter what the time zones, children function according to their own inner time clocks.

Bring blankies, teddy bears, or other sleep soothers but DO NOT bring your one and only MOST precious ones. An irreplaceable teddy left in the ladies room of

Chicago's O'Hare Airport is just that — irreplaceable. Agree upon lesser-valued items for travel purposes, or even better prevention: have duplicates. Consider excising a small square of a favorite quilt (one probably in tatters by now anyway) to take with you, tucking the rest around the half-bald stuffed poodle being left behind.

Label anything you do bring so that it can find its way back again, but only with address or contact numbers, no names. (When an adult calls a child by name the child can be confused, thinking this might be a safe person. Ditto the reason for not displaying names on visible luggage tags.)

Pin or tie treasured items to coat sleeves or back packs. I still remember the ride home when we did not discover that Teddy had headed one direction on the ferry across Puget Sound while we had headed the other. That was a l-o-n-g and nap-less car ride.

FOOD AND EATING

Pack simple, non-messy snacks. Roasted almonds, granola bars, and boxes of apple juice are good: sticky fruit leather, purple grape juice, or salty peanuts and meltable chocolates are not. Bring portable wipes (moistened paper towels in a plastic bag work fine).

On the other hand, an entire Piggly-Wiggly does not contain enough snacks for a multi-day train trip. Those energy-gobbling, time-consuming walks to the diner and back are worth every dollar.

Use meals as breaks. Begin driving at 3 a.m. with everyone still in pajamas and asleep (except, of course, the driver). The first stop of the day can be a mid-morning breakfast/brunch. Children dress in pre-selected outfits while crouched in the backseat or hopping from foot to foot in a restroom stall (with an adult present).

Tip: Always keep a change of clothes in carry-ons or within reach.

TOILETING

Never overlook a toileting opportunity. Trot to restrooms before getting into a car, bus, train, or plane. Get everyone to at least try. Enough said.

ENTERTAINMENT

What to do — in the airport, in the car, onboard a train, or bus? Prevention, remember? Pack a travel bag — one per child. A mix of old (familiar or favorites) and new (special and surprises) is best.

Purchase small child-size backpacks (wheeled ones for longer trips) so each child may carry his own (at least at first). In the car, a double grocery bag or empty box stationed by each seat keeps crayons, books, and papers at hand.

Hand out new items at intervals: after every hour of peaceful travel; when a meal was eaten without mayhem; at the beginning of each new segment of a trip. In desperate situations, dole out single crayons to celebrate every 10-15 minutes of peace (I considered four children in the same car a **desperate situation**).

Magnetic board games (fewer missing pieces); reusable stickers — especially those with backgrounds (houses, forests, or farmyards) to rearrange or create stories; and origami paper (learn how to fold a drinking cup before the trip) are great choices.

A clipboard substitutes as a portable desk, while drawing pads are preferable to loose sheets. Washable markers and crayons (avoid pointed pens and pencils); erasable slates, magic pictures that appear when being rubbed or dot-to-dot art and mazes all keep minds whirring — instead of fingers poking, feet probing, or voices whining.

All noisemaking devices need to have earphones (be sure that volumes are kept at safe levels). A hand-held CD player, DVDs, or storybooks with follow-along texts will help the miles and hours fly by, but do consider banning these for at least part of each trip to enjoy the experience of the journey.

PEOPLE GAMES

Play together. Variation of "I Spy" can focus attention on what is outside the window: who can spot a black cow; find a house with a smoking chimney; or call out first sightings of South Dakota license plates or chrome hood ornaments.

"Twenty-questions" can go on for miles: "Is it an animal?" "Did this person live in America?" "Can the item fit in a toaster?"

Create a family quest. One mom and her daughter chose a theme of *pies* and asked those who they met about their favorite pies; gathered secret, family recipes; and ordered pie at every new restaurant, enjoying food for both mind and body.

SONG

Don't forget family sing-a-longs. For the musically challenged, a tape or CD can carry the tunes while everyone else belts out whatever notes they please.

"Jingle Bells" in July is fine — if those are the only words everyone knows. We have crooned "Home on the Range" to fields of Canadian sheep, sung "This Land is My Land" to crowded interstate commuters, and warbled about "little puffer bellies all in a row" to the bafflement of sunbathing chipmunks and stream-dwelling frogs.

GETTING THERE

Remember that **getting there** is vacation time, too. The patchwork pattern of fields seen through a plane's window, the change from a city's hot asphalt to cool mountain air, the spicy scent of pines inhaled through open car windows, or the brown squiggle of a river spied beneath a 200-foot-high train trestle, all transform travel. Provide each child with an inexpensive camera to record her version of the trip.

On an all-day drive, check into a motel with a pool and cool down with a swim. Buy bread, cheese, and apples and then explore a park over lunch; collect postcards, sand samples, or sugar packets; give in to fruit stands and eat oranges, peaches, or cherries next to the trees where they ripened. One family read *Miss Rumphius* beforehand, and scattered their own lupine seeds throughout several states.

Stay flexible. Viewing a buffalo herd up close, lured by a sign en route, was at least as memorable as our planned visit to Glacier Park.

*Let **there** be **here**, and you will enjoy*
***getting there** as much as **being there**.*

RESOURCE: A great source for travel toys and equipment is Madallie.com. Compiled by two moms, this online children's travel store will inspire your own creativity as well as provide great choices and supplies to make getting there fun for everyone.

Hard Topics

*Challenges come in many forms: some of them we can
anticipate (like providing information about awkward topics
such as sex), but many we cannot (divorce, separation,
death, or illness) and they change everything.
What happens when our safe family cocoon collapses?
Resilience comes from life experiences — it is not
something we can hand out like lollipops.
Balancing the need to protect our children beside the
needed strength that only their experiences can provide is a
daunting task. Some HARD TOPICS along with suggestions
for how to face, cope, or simply live with them:
Sex Talk • Time to Grieve • Make It Better
What If . . . Is Something Wrong with My Child?*

More About Sex:
Sex and Sexuality

Situation: Sex and Sexuality

While taking her bath, a five year old stands up, then giggles and drapes a washcloth over her crotch saying, "I have to cover my peanuts."

In a kindergarten classroom a group of children sit down to a pretend breakfast. A little girl joins them, reaching under her t-shirt to pull out the baby doll she had placed there. "I just had a baby boy," she says. The others nod and continue their play.

A mom walks through the door carrying a clean pile of pants and socks, surprising two brothers busy comparing their penises.

Solution: It Isn't About Size

Of the three situations, which one would you most want to avoid? The first one is cute and funny, the second seems rather sweet and endearing, but the third one tiptoes a bit too close to a topic most of us don't like to have to deal with: sexuality. It is one thing to name body parts or even to tell a child that there is a baby growing in mommy's tummy, but when we face having to talk about what people should or should not do with certain body parts, things get awkward.

THEY NOTICE

One thing is clear from all three examples: Children notice that people have different body parts and they are curious about how those parts work and why they are different. What do children need to know and when and how do we go about telling them? As with most things — slow but steady is a good approach.

JUST THE FACTS, PLEASE

There are developmental stages in learning about sexuality. Most of us are either tempted to say nothing or to go overboard with too much information. Move from simple to detailed when describing body parts and functions. (Doo-dah, booby, and wee-wee are not the terms I am referring to here.) For younger children words such as penis, vagina, and breast are fine. If a child says, 'peanuts' repeat the correct word and maybe add, "A boy has a penis and girl has a vagina." Why boys and girls have different parts can be explained in increasing detail, later.

When a child of four or five asks where babies come from, she does not need an advanced biology lesson. Saying, "Babies grow inside their mommy's bodies in a special place called a uterus," covers the facts that she can handle.

The same questions posed by a six year old might need a different answer. "A man's penis places sperm inside a woman's vagina. When the sperm combine with tiny eggs inside the woman's body, a baby begins to grow."

Still older school-age children can handle additional details — terms such as sexual intercourse, semen, and pubic hair become appropriate information.

WHAT TO SAY?

One mom remembers her shock at realizing that she had not explained menstruation to her 13-year-old daughter. This was a conscientious mom, but the years had passed more quickly than she had expected. (Fortunately for both of them, her daughter was a late-bloomer, and their talk managed to precede the event — barely!)

It is easy to let the months or years slip by without sharing necessary information — especially if the topic is one you find embarrassing. This is where **steady** comes in. Making sex less of an unmentionable topic means keeping discussions ongoing. Your nervousness communicates itself. Frequency will help to raise everyone's comfort level. Stay matter-of-of fact. "When a boy's penis gets firm it is called an erection." (Yes, even little boys do have them!)

If your child sees a nursing mother, simply saying, "A mother's body makes milk for her baby," is straightforward and conveys respect for this basic act. To say, "It isn't nice to look," or "Babies should not be fed in public," supports an attitude of shame and makes both the act of nursing and the mother and baby seem immoral.

WHEN AND HOW?

When a child asks a question or seems confused about something she sees or hears, use it as a **teachable moment**. Watching your little girl attempt to stand while peeing could lead to a discussion of the fact that girls don't have penises but have a vagina instead. Pace information to the curiosity your child shows. If she shows no interest or she covers her ears and says, "Yuck," — back off. Try again later.

Those brothers found comparing penises present a perfect opportunity to engage in a talk about the importance of keeping private parts covered. Include a brief lesson on touching. "A doctor may need to examine your penis, but no one else needs to touch your penis. Touching should never be kept secret, either." (Are you flinching less at the word penis? See, frequency works!)

An early safety lesson, such as the one above, can be inserted into a discussion without causing undue alarm. Sexual abuse is a reality — and it is not only **stranger danger**. Open discussions will keep adults accessible so that children know they can tell or ask us anything.

Other common ways for conversations to begin are through what is seen or heard in the media, from books, or even something overheard. Start by asking what a child knows or understands. It is important not to assume what a child may know or not know. Fill in needed information and clear up misconceptions. Check on a child's interpretation of information, including your explanations.

Human bodies are beautiful and good. If your family is comfortable with nudity under certain circumstances, explain how those circumstances are unique. It may be fine to step out of the bath and walk down the hall without a towel, but when there are visitors it is not acceptable to do so.

DEFINING VALUES AND DIFFERENCES

Sex education requires real soul-searching. What do you believe is appropriate or not? We can't teach what we can't define. Finding ways to honor your values while teaching children to show respect for others' choices is challenging. Whether your family vacations at a nudist camp or you shudder at so much as a shared bath time, your values are your own and deserve respect. So do others.

Sexuality and sex education breach the tricky territory of personal values. Each of us makes different choices — including sexual choices and children will encounter many different lifestyles.

Does your child have a friend being raised by two mommies? How do you explain cousin Frank's special 'roommate'? Some children will grow up to be homosexuals. Does your daughter know that you would still love her if this were the case? Would your son be able to talk to you about it? The more we make sexual development — including differences — safe to talk about, the more reassured children will feel.

BIG ISSUES — SMALL STEPS

Defining values is only one piece of a very large picture. A stroll down the local toy aisle — from pointy-breasted dolls, to preschooler make-up kits, to muscle-bound plastic heroes — provides children with countless sexual images. Is training little girls to see their sexuality as provocative or encouraging little boys to identify with macho-sexual stereotypes what you want for your child? From stumbling over what to call body parts, to far more serious issues, sex is a topic that we can't ignore.

When Hasbro announced plans to market dolls based on the Pussycat Dolls, a real-life group known for sexualized dance and music, letters from parents convinced them that such dolls would be inappropriate. Our actions, as well as our words, matter.

KEEP AT IT

Appreciating that men and women, or boys and girls, have sexual parts that are different — that some body parts need to be kept private — and that we need to respect as well as enjoy our bodies, are important lessons. We are sexual beings. Give your children a healthy foundation of knowledge and encourage open and ongoing conversations. Keep at it. It will get easier, which is a good thing, since those **show me** bathroom moments are only the beginning.

MORE READING

FOR PARENTS:

The Thinking Parent's Guide to Talking Sense About Sex, Deborah M. Roffman, 2001, Perseus Books Group.

How to Talk to Your Kids About Really Important Things: For Children Four to Twelve, Charles E. Schaefer, Teresa Foy DiGeronimo, 1994, Jossey-Bass Books.

FOR CHILDREN:

What's the BIG Secret?, by Laurie Krasny Brown, Marc Brown, 1997, Little Brown & Co.

Heather has Two Mommies, Leslea Newman, 1989, Allyson Publications.

Keeping Safe:
"Make It All Better"

Situation: How to Protect Our Children

"Mom-mee! M-o-om-mee!" When my son's cries pierced the night, I'd dash to his room. His small body would tremble as he sat drenched in sweat, tangled in his Lion King® sheets. Wrapping my arms around him, I would hold him in my lap, smoothing damp hair from his face.

"Calm down. You are safe. Mommy's here." The bad dream would retreat; at 2 a.m. my arms could bring comfort when the night had become too dark.

When my daughter was a preschooler and a swollen sore throat brought tears to her cheeks, I would rock her, holding her fevered head against my chest, "It will feel better soon. Mama will hold you and it will be all better." Her tears would dry and she would fall asleep in my arms.

Yesterday, as I scooped up my granddaughter, after she had slipped on a wet floor, I could feel her body relax as I stroked her back and she rested her head on my shoulder. "There. There. It's all better now."

*As I comforted her I thought about **making it all better**. **Making it all better** is an adult's task. Remembering back, I also realized that scary dreams, painful throats, and slippery floors were only the beginning.*

Solution

MAMA BEAR

How can we **make it all better**? Fierce growls, bared teeth, and several hundred pounds of an infuriated mama bear might send a clear message to those who come too near her baby bear cubs, but how can we mama and papa humans do as good a job of protecting our young?

Some dangers can be prevented: poisons put out of reach; sore throats and nightmares soothed; but what about the rest? What kind of vigilance does it take when the nightly news spatters blood across our slipper-clad feet or Mother Nature rages outside our doors?

How do we **make it all better**; create a safe harbor; become the safe refuge from life's stormy seas?

THE BIG APRON

Years ago, an instructor in my teacher-training program, Madeline Justus, told our class an earthquake story. She had been with a group of preschoolers when the quake occurred. She described reassuring the children and guiding them out of the shaking building to safety.

Did she know that they would be safe? "No." Was she scared? "Yes."

"There are times when we adults must hold our **big aprons** wide," she said.

That image stayed with me. There are times when children need shielding, when we stand on our wobbly grown-up legs with our knees knocking and do our best to hold that **big apron** wide.

A lecture given by Dr. Diane Levin on media violence and the early sexualization of children, recalled Ms. Justus's story to mind. Dr. Levin described the adults that children typically encounter in the colorful world of bouncing cartoon characters or eye-rolling television moppets, as falling into three categories: incompetent; in the way; or just plain idiots. Where are the role models of adults who can be trusted; turned to in a crisis; relied upon; the ones who can **make it all better**? I thought of Ms. Justus's words and wondered, "Where are the **big aprons** out there?"

Remember that moment in the "Sound of Music" when Captain Von Trapp and his new bride stood together, facing the soldiers sent to arrest him? Can you picture the invisible **big apron** the Captain and Maria held, over the roof of that silent car as their children trembled beside them?

What kind of role models did children see with their afternoon cookies and milk today? Do we have our **big aprons** ready? Here are three Ps that might help us to **make it all better** — **protect**, **persist**, and **protest**.

• *PROTECT*

When 'all the other kids' get to play R-rated video games or head to the cinema complex, lining up to see the latest car-crashing, gun-blazing box office hit — what do we do?

Some of us refuse to join the stampede, no matter what 'all the other kids' get to do. Popularity is not a parenting skill. Chances are 'all the other kids' will evaporate into one (or none), upon inquiry.

> *Protect: means keeping safe. Limits protect.*

PERSIST

On the other hand, destroying all of the spinning wheels in the kingdom could not prevent *Sleeping Beauty* from getting her finger pricked. Even if we throw away every television in our kingdom, there are several next door. We go beyond **protect** when we **persist**.

Instead of turning videos and movies into forbidden fruit, some of us choose to grab our own bags of popcorn. We dip into the buttery morsels as glass shatters, tires screech, and bodies pile up on screen; and smile through the reassuring squeeze we offer when that small hand finds ours in the dark. Afterwards we talk. We invite thinking:

"What did you think of that man using his gun to kill the other man?"
"What about that house getting bombed? Were you scared?"

And we reassure:

"That was scary for me too. But we are safe and I am right here."
And you are there, were there — and will be there.

When fierce winds, pounding rain, or trembling earth shakes us to our foundations
—— as we huddle in darkened homes, await rescue on rooftops, or must flee walls
of rushing water — we are there beside our own children, or those children who
may be beside us in that moment. We do our best to reassure and spread those
aprons wide — no matter how battered or in tatters they may have become.

*Persist: means **being there**, available — present — always.*

BEING THERE

Dr. Levin tells another story, one of preschoolers lying beside their toppled block
towers, playing dead — reenacting the evening news reports of America's
Oklahoma City bombing. How could their teacher intervene? Should she forbid
the children to play their grisly game? Would that **make it all better**? No.
This teacher recognized it was time to spread her **big apron**. She joined the
children in their play, taking the role of a doctor, going around making the fallen
children better again. Why? Because she was the adult and that is what we
adults do — we **make it all better**.

Maybe in the real world we can only join our tears to those of children left
orphaned by war or disaster, but for those children watching the nightly news
beside us; trusting us; counting upon us: we must be there, our **big aprons** at
the ready. That's **persistence**.

PROTEST

Adults make all kinds of choices. When buying a lunch box, nightgown, or
backpack we can think about the characters depicted; the movie selections we

agree to and the messages we send with each purchase or selection. It is our task to assess the toys on a store's shelves — then use (or refuse to use) our pocketbooks to voice our conclusions; affirm our values; and make the world **all better** — for our children and others, as well.

It is also our job to make the decisions that will affect the kind of world all children inherit. Taking our responsibilities as stewards of the world's resources to heart, we teach our children to tread lightly on this fragile earth through our lifestyles and actions because these, too, are part of our job.

Protest: means living our values and matching actions to words. We want our children to think about and question what they see. They learn by watching what we do.

Do you write to the *friendly* multi-national toy store, the *friendly* multi-national toy makers, or the *friendly* megabucks movie studios and television stations and tell them what you think of the big-breasted wrestling dolls for sale on aisle three; or the winged cartoon character who makes mayhem look harmless over the Saturday morning cornflakes; or the lack of G-rated movies in this week's newspaper listings? Do you write to those in power when environmental issues are at stake? Our voices do get heard, especially when their numbers grow. One voice multiplied by millions makes a mighty sound — too loud to ignore.

PARENTING Ps

A GROWN-UP CHALLENGE

Protect — Persist — Protest. When bad things invade — whether a winter virus, movie mayhem, or a real-life tragedy — we adults must spread our arms, pull out our **big aprons** and **make it all better** — because that is our job. That is what adults do — even when the nightmares become real.

Protect:
Set sensible limits
that protect.

Persist:
Always 'be there'
for your child.

Protest:
What affects any of us
— affects us all.

A Time to Cry:
The Grieving Process

Situation: A Time to Cry — The Grieving Process

"We're worried about Janine hitting her classmates the past few weeks. She's
begun hitting her little sister, too, and we don't know what to do about it."
Janine's parents sat in small chairs across the table from Ms. Lui, Janine's teacher.
"Is there anything different going on at home?" Ms. Lui asked.

"No, everything is the same as usual," Janine's parents said. After talking over
ways to respond to Janine's hitting, her parents gathered their coats to leave.
Janine's mom said, "Thank you so much for giving us some new discipline ideas.
On top of helping my Mom go through Dad's things since his death last month,
I've felt too overwhelmed to cope with Janine's recent hitting."

Solution: The Misbehavior Link

Uh oh! Reverse the tape. What was that? Grandfather died last month?
'Everything' is definitely **not** the 'same as usual'.

It is easy to be so caught up in our own struggles when facing life crises that we
fail to recognize their connection to a child's behavior. The loss of a family
member, friend, or even a pet can bring about significant changes. One child may

begin to wet the bed, another refuse to eat, and another, like Janine, may hurt others.

Improved discipline is not likely to resolve unresolved grief.

CHILDREN'S GRIEVING

Grieving is a process that both children and adults experience, but children do not grieve in straightforward ways. They may **act out** in ways that seem unrelated.

When Aunt Lizzie dies, little Julio may tear the pages of his *Curious George* book, his sister Juanita may complain of stomachaches and not do her homework, and their cousin Bonita may refuse to do her chores or pick up her toys.

Without words to name their feelings, children speak through actions.

DEATH IS PERMANENT

Grappling with death is difficult for all of us, but for children its meaning changes with their age and developmental level.

Death is permanent. This is a concept that children under five cannot grasp. The morning that our goldfish floated to the top of its bowl was a landmark for one of our children in understanding this concept.

Our five-year-old daughter became very upset over the death of this goldfish, but it was not a simple matter of racing to the pet store to get a replacement as we had done when previous fish had left this world. This fish was gone — forever. And that was the real meaning of this loss for her. Forever.

At that moment, by understanding that this fish would never swim, eat its fish flakes, or wiggle its tail again, our daughter had begun to understand death's permanence.

DEATH IS UNIVERSAL

Another of our daughters, at the age of four, had not grasped this idea of permanence. When we drove past the local cemetery on our way to her preschool, she would smile and point to it saying, "That is where the dead people live," as if we were passing an interesting apartment complex. To her **death** had no permanence, nor did she understand that it was the end of **living**.

She also could not understand the universal nature of death. In her mind, death was reserved for those people 'living' within the cemetery gates.

DEATH BY ANY OTHER NAME . . .

Young children are very literal. Referring to **losing** a person may lead a child to believe that the person will later be **found**. Describing death as 'going to sleep' can associate sleep with death, creating new fears and problems.

Use simple words to describe death. "Granny died last night. She is not alive anymore."

ALLOW FEELINGS

When a child feels sad, distracting him or telling him the person is in a 'better place' can undermine grieving. Feelings are a messy business, but the grieving process cannot be hurried. It is only by going **through grieving** that we can emerge on the other side and **begin healing**.

Children may become angry, withdrawn, or even act as if they are oblivious to what is going on. This last reaction is a sort of 'frozen' state, where a child acts silly or unconcerned because the enormity of his feelings overwhelms him.

It is important to let a child know that any feeling, no matter how unpleasant, is safe to talk about with a parent or caring adult. If your own grief is too acute, ask a trusted friend or family member to be available to your child.

WAVES OF FEELING

Grieving affects our bodies as well as our minds and emotions. Feelings of grief are often experienced as waves that move through the body. When we try to stop the wave, it becomes stuck inside us. Our throats squeeze tight and words can't get past. We may feel pressure in our chests, against our eyes, or at our foreheads.

Other times the wave seems to twist around our hearts and we truly feel **heartbreak** as if the pain is **breaking** our hearts apart. Children experience these feelings too, but don't understand them.

The grieving process comes in cycles and children need breaks from its intensity. Planning times to run at the park, go for a swim, or play catch in the backyard will give a child needed relief.

HEALING TEARS

When we allow the waves of grief to wash through us, they often flow out as tears. These tears are healing, containing toxins that our bodies are shedding. Not everyone cries to process their grief, but understanding the need to allow these waves of feeling to flow out of our bodies is important. If we do not honor this process the sadness can lodge inside us, trapped like glowing embers. A later loss can fan these embers into new flames, that grow bigger the longer they have smoldered.

Allowing a child to see or share in one's tears is healing for both the adult and the child. There is nothing weak or shameful about our tears.

We model grieving just as we do other things.

SAYING GOOD-BYE

We all need ways to say good-bye after a death. Over the years, raising four children meant saying good-bye to a wide assortment of pets. There were gerbils (some had to be kept in the freezer if the ground was too hard to dig a hole when they chose to leave us), numerous fish (including the ones that died when one child tried out a new wooden hammer on the aquarium glass), and, of course, various dogs and cats.

For each burial we would gather wherever my husband had dug the correct-sized hole, and place the pet, contained in its cardboard box, baggie, or sack, into the ground.

Often our pets got 'planted' in the garden so they could become part of the new life that would grow there. In the wonderful children's book *The Tenth Good Thing About Barney* by Judith Viorst, thinking that his beloved cat, Barney, will now help make plants grow, ("a pretty nice job for a cat"), helps this little boy to begin to accept the loss of his pet.

MEMORIES

As part of our pet burials we would talk about how much we loved that particular fish, rat, cat, or dog. We shared our stories: the time one dog walked across the newly painted porch and made yellow paw prints all over the hall carpet; the bravery of the cat that sent a visiting Rottweiler cowering behind its owner; or the way a certain rat enjoyed taking rides nestled inside a shirt collar (not mine!). These stories brought laughter, sighs, and tears and helped us to say good-bye.

Sharing our memories makes losses easier to bear.

FUNERAL/BURIAL — CHILD'S CHOICE

The decision of if or how a child should participate in a funeral ceremony or burial is an individual one. Allowing the child to choose to attend, but not insisting if he or she refuses, is best. If a child does choose to take part, be sure to describe what will take place — including the possibility that adults may be crying, so that the child will not find this alarming.

Allow children to help with planning, such as choosing a scarf or clothing item for the deceased to wear, picking out pictures to display, or music to be played at the service.

Make arrangements for an adult to be available to take a child away from the services if need be, whether the child becomes too distressed, or simply cannot be still for such a long time.

PROCESSING GRIEF

Whether the child attends the funeral or not, make time for grieving. Lighting a candle, saying a prayer, or going for a walk in a favorite place that brings the loved one to mind can help. Looking through family photo albums or displaying a collection of shells from a shared vacation can bring back memories of times spent together. Draw pictures, mold clay, or create collages to express emotions, thus removing the need for words. Children orphaned by AIDS find solace by creating a memory box, often with the help of a dying parent.

MAGICAL THINKING

Young children believe in 'magic' and their thinking reflects that. Make time to be available to listen, giving a child an opportunity to tell something that may be troubling him, such as a belief that Auntie died because he had called her a 'meany'. This gives adults a chance to help clear up such confusing thoughts. Take cues from the child and do not push. Share your own thoughts and feelings to encourage a child to share hers.

ANNIVERSARIES

Grieving takes time. When a loved one dies, special dates will bring back renewed sadness. Acknowledge the anniversary of a death, a first holiday without the person's presence, or the deceased person's birthday or other special date in some way. This helps healing proceed.

GET HELP

If behavior changes continue for several weeks, interfere with daily living, or affect the child's life in deeper ways, seek outside help.

A wonderful book for both adults and older children is *Tear Soup* by Pat Schwiebert and Chuck DeKlyen, in which the authors use the making of tear soup as a metaphor for the grieving process. When we understand the nature of grief as a process, we can honor the time needed to heal.

There is often a connection between feelings of loss or sadness and a child's misbehavior, especially when those feelings remain unprocessed.

Deep healing, not discipline may be what is truly needed.

BOOKS AND FURTHER RESOURCES

Britain, Lori. *My Grandma Died*. Seattle, WA: Parenting Press, 2003.
This is a simple book in which a child talks about his feelings and
    compares them to similar previous feelings.

Cohn, Janet. *I had a Friend Named Peter.* New York: William Morrow &
    Co., 1987.
A child is helped to cope with the accidental death of a friend.

Schwiebert, Pat, & DeKlyen, Chuck. *Tear Soup*. Portland, Oregon:
    Grief Watch, 2001.
This book does a beautiful job of exploring the grief process and has
    extensive resources listed in its appendix.

Visna, Judith. *Saying Goodbye to Daddy.* Morton Grove, IL: A. Whitman,
    1991.
This book addresses the immediate needs after the death of a parent and
    through the funeral and first weeks.

Viorst, Judith. *The Tenth Good Thing About Barney*. New York: Aladdin
    Books, 1987.
A Bernard Wilets Film video (also available in book form)
This story deals with the loss of a pet.

Yolen, Jane. *Granddad Bill's Song*. New York: Putnam and Grosset,
    1994.
A child listens to others' memories, sharing his own.

For many more resources on a variety of topics go to the Dougy center
    web site: www.dougy.org. The Dougy center is devoted to helping
    children deal with death and grief.

What If . . .
Is Something Wrong
With My Child?

Situation

Carolyn says that her daughter, Caitlin, has two speeds: Fast and asleep! *What she doesn't admit out loud, is her worry that Caitlin's fast speed might foreshadow 'hyper' speed, as in Attention Deficit 'Hyperactivity' Disorder (ADHD), something she's watched her own brother struggle with.*

Joseph gets frustrated when 18-month-old Colin doesn't respond to being called by his name. Is Colin ignoring his dad, will he outgrow this behavior, or could it be something is wrong?

Bob and Juana can't get their son, Abraham, potty-trained. Abraham, age four, refuses to use the toilet, instead soiling his pants. His parents fear that something may be wrong with Abraham but instead of speaking their fears aloud, they blame each other for not being firm enough or accuse one another of being inconsistent.

Solution: Secret Fears

Stories like the ones above could go on and on. Parents worry that a child isn't walking or talking. They worry about how much or how little gets eaten and spend fortunes on educational toys. They also deny their concerns, get angry if others suggest possible problems, or reassure one another that 'it's just a phase.' What gets tricky is deciding when a common concern indicates an uncommon condition.

ADHD AND 'WAIT-AND-SEE'

Caitlin may turn out to simply be a child with a lot of energy. As she ages and enters elementary school she may retain that high energy and continue to need lots of large muscle and outdoor experiences. The truth is that lots of children show symptoms of ADHD-like behavior in their early years because the mechanisms that help control impulses (including movement control), or that support the ability to focus, are still under development in young brains.

On the other hand, children do, in fact, show early symptoms of later problems, among them ADHD. Difficulty with focusing, learning to control one's emotional responses (tantrums, aggression), or to moderate movement and adjust to changes are best responded to in these early years with consistency and skill building, along with a wait-and-see attitude. Since ADHD is usually not diagnosed until age six or older, this wait-and-see approach makes sense. But if a child's problems do not diminish with age, school and/or social skill issues increase, or if your child begins to feel that he is a 'bad kid' — then do seek help.

EARLY INTERVENTION

This wait-and-see approach is not appropriate for all concerns in the early years. Colin's lack of response to his name, if it is persistent and part of a pattern of no or minimal social connectedness, could be a red flag for autism, even as early as one to one-and-a-half years of age. In fact, research has shown that this particular lack of response to one's name can be a powerful early autism indicator.

Another explanation for non-responsive behavior could be hearing-related. A child with ear infections may have intermittent hearing loss or eardrum damage from scarring. Hearing problems can lead to disruptive behavior, whether from missing out on directions or out of frustration with not being understood.

Hearing and speech problems often go together. Speech is hard to master if what is heard is intermittent or inaccurate. By the age of 24-months, two-thirds of what a child says should be understandable to strangers, and by 36-months it should be closer to 90 percent.

Other children will not compensate for a child they cannot understand (whereas a parent, and brothers or sisters will supply words and decode a child's mispronunciations). A child who is not understood has more trouble making friends, interacting in play, and is at risk of becoming aggressive (hitting, biting, pushing), or of becoming withdrawn (discouraged and giving up). With even a few weeks or months of therapy, language skills can improve dramatically.

Hearing and speech problems, as well as potential autism all need early intervention to enable a child to reach her full developmental potential. The earlier help is provided, in all of these different situations, the better the success of remediation — and the less chance that negative damage will result.

A good rule of thumb is: *when in doubt— check it out.*

LETTING GO

Abraham's parents, worried about his toileting difficulties, may be the first ones who need to 'let go.' Anxious parents or teachers communicate their anxiety to children. A child, who is slow to develop a life skill such as toileting, could take even longer to succeed when feeling pressured to do so.

Since much of toileting is about control, a child who feels overpowered by adults may seek control by withholding his waste. Children will endure painful constipation rather than 'give in.' If your child, like Abraham, resists using the toilet and soils or wets his pants instead, the first approach is to look for ways to help him feel appropriate power in his life.

A good way to give children a sense of control over their lives is to offer limited choices. Offering a choice between orange juice or apple juice is an example of a limited choice. Offering him anything at all to drink and then proceeding to say

"No" to requests for soda or milkshakes, results in frustration and sets up power struggles. On the other hand, a limited choice with its acceptable options helps him to feel empowered.

Having said all of that, a four year old who is soiling his pants (or a child of this age or older who is bed-wetting) most of the time, may need medical evaluation. There are both encopresis (the name for soiling) and enuresis (bed-wetting) specialists.

Something as simple as having a child blow bubbles with a small jar of bubble solution while sitting on the potty can help move things along (so to speak) as it is impossible to blow and squeeze at the same time. Diet changes such as the addition of extra fiber and fluids, or medical intervention such as stool softeners can also be effective.

Although there are numerous options to help master bed-wetting, it is often something that a child will need to outgrow. Nonetheless, a medical evaluation will rule out other concerns.

CHECK IT OUT

Although early intervention is important, for most parents just how 'early' is 'early enough' underscores the critical bottom-line. A good early childhood program can help determine the developmental status of a child. Well-trained caregivers are alert to potential warning signs, as well as informed about the availability of local resources.

The bottom-line answer is that **you** are your child's first and best advocate. If you're concerned — get the information you need. Whether your child needs help or is simply developing at a different pace — you will know what to do.

And remember:
When in doubt — check it out.

Universal Tools

Whatever the problem affecting child or adult,
certain basic tools will help.
Here are a few you don't want to do without:

Routines and Structure
Life Skills: From Time Out to Cool Off
More Life Skills: Family Meetings
Putting It All Together
Kind and Firm: Eye Drops

Routines and Structures: Structure in Our Lives — What? Why? How?

Situations: From Chaos to Crisis — Structure to the Rescue

BACKFIRING BEDTIME

I wanted my daughter to respond to her own body's rhythms by allowing her to fall asleep when she was ready to do so. This plan has backfired. Often it is midnight before she falls asleep — most often on the sofa or in front of the television.

I am more than ready for bed by 10 p.m. She is getting too heavy to carry to her room, and I have no time to myself. How can I turn this around without a battle?

DIRTY DISH DISASTER

My partner and I agreed that our sons (5 and 6 years) are old enough to help clear the table after dinner. The problem is that if they don't do so, she ignores it and then tells me I am making it into too big an issue if I persist in trying to get them to do it.

I am very frustrated, as well as stuck with everyone else's mess.

A CAVE-DWELLING FUTURE

We took our four year old to the museum. He ran up and down the aisles, grabbed at the sculptures, and tugged on the displayed wall hangings. As soon as we got home, I sent him to his room for a time-out.

I am still upset. We can't take him anywhere. I feel like we might as well become cave-dwellers!

Solution: Structure to the Rescue

Structure is something that may make people squirm, but all of the above scenarios are about **structure** — or its absence.

Structure is a combination of three things: **Routines and Habits**; **Needs and Expectations**; and **Follow-Through**. Each of these is a component for developing resilient families.

• Routines/Habits

Things that occur on a regular basis, at a regular time, or in a consistent way are **routines**. Eating breakfast and going to bed are daily **routines**.

Routines become **habits** when they happen often enough to be done without conscious thought. When I get ready for bed each night, I place my glasses on my dresser. Same place, same time, same action, over and over and over again. That is a **routine** that has matured (along with my eyesight), into a **habit**.

When a child enters the house and places his coat on a coat peg — day after day, same place, same action — it has become a **habit**. These are useful habits.

When another child tosses his coat on the floor as soon as he walks through that door — day after day — he, too, has a **habit**, but not a very desirable one.

Habits are a bit like rabbits: good or bad, they multiply.

THE BRAIN CONNECTION

The reason **habits** and **routines** go together is wired into our brains. Brains are programmed to regard things that are new, different, or unusual as suspicious, which can result in resistance.

When a child is asked to do something, even something familiar, it can still bring resistance if the request is infrequent or inconsistent. Establishing **routines** requires patience, planning, and persistence, while turning **routines** into **habits** takes lots of **follow-through**.

STARTING A ROUTINE

The more involved everyone is in the planning phase, the higher the level of cooperation will be. The mom with the midnight marvel who won't go to bed might not get a cheer for suggesting a fixed bedtime, but working on a plan for a bedtime routine can ease the transition. Here's a glimpse:

"Before bed we need to do what?"
"Brush teeth, read stories, and pray."

Great! Now use markers, crayons, or magazine cut-outs to illustrate this plan with: pictures of smiles or toothbrushes; books; and praying hands, prayer rugs, or meditation bells. Let your child use this chart as a guide to walk through the nightly **routine**, ending up with her in bed.

Sleeping will be up to her, but getting her there in a consistent way through a nightly **routine** will become easier as her brain ceases to find the process novel. Over time the **routine** will become a **habit** and part of a child's natural body rhythm, but now one the whole family will find restful.

ADVANCE WARNING

Prepare the brain for change. The parent, who wants the children to clear a table, can ask them who will clear the leftovers and who will stack the dishes. Done **before** the meal is over, this will remind them of the task; reinforce the establishment of the routine; and the choice gives each child a feeling of empowerment. It is also a great way to avoid power struggles (negative power) and to gain cooperation (as well as a cleared table).

NEEDS AND EXPECTATIONS

The family preparing to hole up in their cave rather than take their child anywhere ever again, will find another type of **structure** helpful. The missing **structure** in their museum adventure may have been that of communicating the **needs and expectations** of the situation ahead of time.

For very young children or a first time experience, a direct explanation is needed:

"The museum exhibits are fragile. It is not Okay to touch the things on display. We must only look at them." (Be sure to include the desired behavior — not just the don'ts.)

Once a child is four or older, he or she has probably gone out into public enough to be able to respond to questions instead of being told:

"When we are at the museum, how do we need to act?"

Give clues within the question:
"Is running allowed?"
"How do we move inside a museum?"
"What are we allowed to touch?"

The value of asking such questions, rather than droning out the rules, is that by responding a child demonstrates both knowledge and understanding (which makes it hard to pretend later that he didn't hear or doesn't know the expectations). This is a very handy feature!

FOLLOW-THROUGH

The final element of structure is that old 'do what you say you will do'. This gets tricky when we meet with resistance and disappointment (a/k/a — a tantrum). The somewhat grim truth is that 'parenting' and 'popular' are not synonyms.

Let's be honest; if there were a possibility that fussing, whining, or acting incompetent might get us out of doing a task — well, wouldn't we all try to get out of unappealing tasks if we thought we could? (Alright, someone out there is saying "Not me," but the rest of us won't invite you to OUR birthday parties — so there!)

The point is that if we want children to **believe** what we say, we have to **mean** what we say. It also means that we need to **be careful of what we say**.

The biggest danger here is **saying** what we are going to **make someone else do** (an unlikely possibility at best). Better to stick with what you can control, namely, **your own actions**.

WHAT WILL <u>YOU</u> DO?

If the table doesn't get cleared, have a contingency plan that focuses on what YOU will do.

Perhaps you agreed that the television wouldn't go on until after the table is cleared. That means: YOU turn off the set while saying, "The table isn't cleared." YOU stay calm. YOU act.

If this does not work and your child chooses to sulk instead of doing the task, continue to stay calm. Breathe. Give him a reasonable amount of time to comply, but **no further reminders**. Then clear the table yourself and the **television stays off**.

If (ha! when) there are complaints, assure your child that you are confident he will remember to do his job tomorrow and be able to enjoy his programs then.

Whose behavior did you control? YOURS. Who chose NOT to clear the table? HE did. Will he clear the table tomorrow? Probably.

Follow-through nurtures habits.

FLEXIBILITY

Successful **structure** has some of the same qualities as a good building. When the night's routine gets rattled, it should be able to bend without crumbling.

Bedtime after a birthday party may be an hour or more off or some nights there may be no time for a story.

Habits can falter without disintegrating. Missing one night of tooth brushing does not mean a denture savings account is needed.

If **needs** change or **expectations** have to be altered, the walls of our life's structure should not tumble. A museum visit can be shortened if a child becomes overtired or hungry.

When **follow-through** turns into a power struggle, it can serve as a warning that the basic structure may need shoring up. Check that it is YOUR actions YOU are controlling.

Sweet dreams.
Happy travels.
Tidy tables.

SUPPORT AND FREEDOM

Routines might seem boring, but they reduce resistance and lead to positive **habits**.

Needs and expectations might seem obvious, but they aren't. They need articulation and reiteration.

Follow-through may feel unpleasant, but is still necessary. Well designed **structure** supports, is flexible, and builds resilience.

ROUTINES TO THE RESCUE

Routines define expectations. They have a sort of extra-terrestrial presence, allowing adults to step back and let the agreed upon routine becomes boss. The **process** of developing a routine is part of the solution. Do not just announce the new routine. Plan it together.

TIP:
Find a pleasant time (not the time of conflict) to do this.

ROUTINE PLANNING REGIMEN

Name YOUR problem:
"I don't like yelling at everyone in the mornings."

Instead of:
"You children cause too many problems by not getting ready quickly each morning."
Which do you think invites greater cooperation?

Ask for HELP: (Children LOVE to help us)
"I need help with this. Are you willing to help me?"

Plan together:
For children under three, talk through a plan while drawing or pasting pictures on a poster.

With older children, ask what needs to happen each morning. List details. Then illustrate it together using magazine pictures (images of a tube of toothpaste, a book, or a bed) or create drawings of your own.

Post it:

Place the Routine Poster in an easily seen spot. Agree to try it for a week or two and then discuss how it is working.

Celebrate improvement:

Perfection is illusive in this world, but notice when things improve. Everyone needs encouragement.

Fine tune:

When problems arise, refer to the routine:

"What is next on our routine?" "Let's check the routine."

Sometimes all that is necessary is to point to the posted routine without saying a word. A child may still object to getting dressed or ready for bed, but she will also feel a sense of control and pride that she remembered the routine.

Example of a Routine Chart:

Time-Out —
How It is Abused

Typically Time-Out is . . .

• A new name for punishment.

One child hits her playmate. Mother marches over and tells the child to "TAKE A TIME-OUT!" Although the words "AND SUFFER" remain unspoken, they reverberate in the air. Children hear the unspoken **suffer** loud and clear.

• Used as a threat.

"Bobby, do you want to have to take a time-out?" Again, the unspoken message is that Bobby better change what he is doing or he will **suffer** for it. Is a suffering child your goal? Is fear the means by which we want children to learn acceptable behavior?

• The only way the adult knows how to respond to a child's misbehavior.

Imagine if the only way a driver could control a car was with the brake pedal. There would be no steering wheel, no way to adjust the gas pedal to reduce speed, and no rearview mirror to monitor traffic. Would you want to drive such a car? If time-out is your only tool, it is time to get a better-equipped vehicle.

• Rarely discussed with children except when they are being sent to it.

It becomes the child's responsibility, with her three year old or younger reasoning ability, to figure out what **time-out** is, why she is being sent there, and how she should act now. Many a child sits on that time-out chair deciding: I am a bad person; no one likes me; or even smiling that she is now the center of attention. Are those the messages we want children to receive?

• A black hole where children disappear.

You plop Mary in the time-out chair and suddenly the baby is throwing up. By the time you have the baby soothed and cleaned up, checked her for signs of illness, and rushed to answer the phone, 20 minutes have slipped past. With a jolt you remember that Mary is still in time-out . . .

• A way to make children *pay* for their misbehavior.

When we focus on controlling a child's behavior, we must win each battle. If we win, what role does that leave for the child? Is time-out a "You Pay — You Stay" corner of your home?

• Only for children.

First of all — who needs the time-out? Sometimes it is the adult. An upset adult placing herself in time-out teaches a powerful lesson. For many children the only response they have ever seen to adult anger is violence. Adult use of time-out provides valuable lessons about life.

Time-Out or Cool-Off —
What It Could/Should Look Like

Positive Time-Out (or Cool-Off) is . . .

• A chance for the child and adult to cool off.

Cooling off takes the heat out of the moment and creates more space between the upset feelings and the typically hurtful reactions of both the child(ren) and adult.

• A place where we go to feel better again.

Feeling better helps us to behave better. Imagine you are eating a luscious ice cream sundae. Your spouse comes by and reminds you how fat you are and says you shouldn't be eating all those calories. Don't you immediately smile and thank him for his helpful words and toss the rest of the sundae to the dog? Probably not. Your spouse will be lucky if you don't toss the ice cream at his head. Discouragement does not motivate anyone.

• A means by which children learn to change disruptive behavior into constructive behavior.

One child lands a blow at a sibling's block tower and prepares for a second jab at the sibling. An adult intervenes sending both children to time-out. Time-out gives both children a break, a chance to regain composure, and provides needed damage control. Sending both children to time-out avoids the need for Solomon-like decisions. Nor does it send out a "Mommy loves me more" message.

• Most effective when the attitude of the adult is kind and firm.
The adult who sees time-out as positive, does not use it as a threat, try to manipulate children with it, or stomp around ordering a child into time-out. Modeling self-control is the adult's responsibility.

• Discussed in advance and the details planned by both adults and children.
An explanation and discussion of positive time-out takes place at a calm moment. Children help decide where time-outs will take place and what objects (cuddly teddy bears, koosh balls, or silky fabrics) or furniture to use in the time-out area. They understand that the time-out area is a place where they may go to help them feel better again.

• Available to a child for as little or as much time as she decides.
Children have control over when they are ready to leave the time-out area. Remember: the goal is for the child to feel better again.

Children want parents and teachers to set reasonable limits, guide and teach them, and follow through with dignity and respect. Positive time-out is a tool that meets these goals even when the adult is correcting misbehavior or helping a child learn more appropriate responses.

Family Meetings:
We've Got to Start Meeting Like This

Situation: We've Got to Start Meeting Like This:
Family Meetings

"She broke my Game Boy®," says Max, glaring at his little sister, Millie.

"Harry took all the cookies. I didn't get any," says Harry's outraged brother, Dan.

"Someone left the drawing art pads out and they got soaking wet in the rain," says mom holding up a soggy Exhibit A.

Solution: It's a Messy Life

When people live together life gets messy. One tool for making coexistence easier is the Family Meeting. Just what a Family Meeting is or is not can be best described by a look at some basic **Dos** and **Don'ts**.

We'll start with the **Don'ts,** because they are probably the most familiar.

FAMILY MEETING: DON'TS

Don't use a Family Meeting:

- As a home-style courtroom.

  Example: "Someone broke Grandma's mirror and we're going to find out whodunit — and punish him (or her)."

- To dictate adult rules.

  Example: "I am sick of picking up everyone's dirty clothes. These are MY laundry rules!"

- Only for crises.

  Example: "That's it! This fighting has to stop! We're having a Family Meeting — right NOW!"

I can almost hear the raised and snarling voices, can't you? To me, these Family Meetings sound about as encouraging as a root canal. Let's move on to the **Dos**.

WHY MEET?

What purpose do Family Meetings serve? There are several. The **Don'ts** make it clear that punishment, blame, crisis encounters, and adult control are not helpful Family Meeting goals.

The **Dos** point us in the direction of respectful interactions, valuing everyone's viewpoint and contribution, and encouraging cooperation as well as learning life skills such as negotiation, creative problem-solving, and how to act upon values. These same results occur whether yours is a single-parent household, two parents with one or a dozen children, or a shared household with related or unrelated adults.

With these things in mind, let's visualize a Family Meeting. There are three basic parts to a Family Meeting: Problem-solving, Appreciations, and Planning Fun Activities.

FAMILY MEETING: DOS

Do use Family Meetings:

- To listen to each person's perspective, ideas, and problems.
  Example: "Max, you wrote 'Game Boy®' on the agenda. Tell us about this problem."
- To teach and model values.
  Example: "We all enjoy treats. How can we show **consideration** for one another? What does **consideration** mean? What would **consideration** look like when we have treats such as cookies available?"

To solve problems:

- Keyword: **Solve**, as in **Solution** (not blame as in punishment or retribution).
  Example: "The drawing pads were ruined in the rainstorm. Who has an idea for a way of remembering to bring all things back inside?"
- To work together regularly. Plan a consistent meeting time (preferably weekly) or schedule the next meeting at the conclusion of the current one:
  Example: "Let's meet every Sunday at lunchtime."
  Or: "What day next week can we meet? Does Monday at dinner work for everyone?"
- To appreciate one another.
  Example: "I appreciate that Harry saved me three chocolate chip cookies."
- To plan fun times together.
  Example: "Whose turn is it to choose Wednesday night's movie?" "Shall we have popcorn? Who wants to make it?"
  Or: "Mark wants ice cream sundaes with crushed Oreos and caramel sauce for his birthday dinner. What other kinds of toppings would we like?

BEFORE WE MEET

As problems occur, they get written on the **Agenda**, followed by the initials of the person for whom this is a concern.

An **Agenda** is a piece of paper posted somewhere in easy access: clipped to a refrigerator magnet; attached to a clipboard or written in a countertop notebook,

or on a kitchen blackboard; or on Post-It® notes tacked to a message board.
Here is a sample:

AGENDA

Game Boy®	Max
Stop hogging cookies	D.
Toys Inside	Mom

Tip: Don't overload the Agenda with adult items. The idea is to
encourage responsibility and participation. If the adults take over,
it's more likely to encourage resistance.

PROBLEM-SOLVING

Begin the meeting by reading through the previous week's notes. Are last week's
problems resolved? Improved? Did the solutions work? Example:

"Last week we decided to put a basket in the back hall for everyone to put toys in
before dinner. How is that working?"
"Sasha won't help put things away!"
"Sasha, what do you think? Are you helping bring the toys in?"

Continue in this way. Seek a new solution or recommit to the previous plan:

Tip 1: Bringing up a topic often helps resolve it.
Tip 2: Deal with only one or two agenda items and save the remainder for future
meetings. Twenty to thirty minutes is a maximum for most families; the younger
the children, the shorter this time frame.
Tip 3: By the time an item comes up for discussion, it is often no longer a
problem.

CONSENSUS

Instead of unanimous agreement for new ideas, seek **consensus**; a plan all can
live with temporarily, even if it wasn't a first choice. Most people are willing to
agree to a limited trial period. Example: "For the next two weeks, would you both
be willing take turns bringing the toys inside?"

Include details. Example:

"Let's write names on the calendar so we'll know whose day it is."

Learning to negotiate solutions is a valuable life skill — far more important than simply getting the toys inside. After reviewing past decisions and making needed adjustments, move on to new items.

FUN, AT LAST

Plan something fun: a trip to the local YMCA for a swim; an activity such as a game of *Monopoly* or *Go Fish*; or a bigger event such as a visit to Uncle Tom and Aunt Mariah's for summer vacation. Be sure that ideas for what to do as well as how to do them are addressed. Here are three ways to do this:

- **Start with a limited selection of possibilities**.
  Example: "We have passes for either the Woodland Park Zoo or the Aquarium. Which would we rather go to this Sunday?"
  Tip: If the zoo visit is chosen, offer those who favored the Aquarium trip a chance to choose the first zoo exhibit, thus promoting inclusion and cooperation.

- **Make a master list of possibilities with everyone contributing ideas.**
  Choose the top three ideas and schedule them as three consecutive outings, so that each person's destination gets selected, encouraging cooperation on **all** the outings.
  Tip: This one teaches 'give and take'.

- **Make individual lists of things each person likes to do.** Then compare lists and circle items that appear on more than one list. Consolidate these into a smaller list from which to chose the outing. Refer back to the lists for future planning.

WE APPRECIATE . . .

End the meeting with **Appreciations**. **Appreciations** provide a formal time for each family member to **acknowledge** one another's **kindnesses**. Here are two ways to ensure that everyone is included:

- Offer an Appreciation for each family member with one person at a time taking a turn.

  Example: Millie — "I appreciate Max for showing me how to use his Game Boy®."

  "I appreciate the chocolate chip cookies Dad made this week."

  "I appreciate Mom for helping me make valentines."

- Alternately, give Appreciations to one family member at a time, with each person taking a turn.

  Example: Millie — "I appreciate Mom's cookies."

  Max — "I appreciate Millie and mom for coming to my soccer game."

  Dad — "I appreciate Mom for helping me get the checkbook balanced."

  Tip: All meetings are not going to be smooth. The Family Meeting provides a way for differences, hurt feelings, and perceived offenses to be dealt with before they can grow. Ending the meeting with Appreciations brings people together and can be healing, especially if tempers got heated during the meeting.

MORE FUN

After Appreciations, consider doing something special together. Our meetings were followed by dessert, a powerful motivator for us. Some families play cards or board games, read stories, listen to music, or exercise together.

Tip: Everyone being gathered makes it easier to glide into a group activity.

LIFE SKILLS

Family Meetings teach life skills. Keeping the drawing pads out of the rain or getting a bite of a chocolate chip cookie is a side benefit. Problems will diminish and stay manageable as skills improve and are used in day-to-day situations.

> *Family Meetings make life a lot less messy —*
> *include everyone — and everyone benefits.*

For a detailed description of how participation will differ by age, read *Positive Discipline for Preschoolers*, chapter "Class Meetings for Preschoolers" (Nelsen, Jane; Erwin, Cheryl; Duffy, Roslyn. Random House, 2007).

MORE FAMILY MEETING TIPS

Build *Family Meeting Skills* like stacking a pyramid, from the bottom up.
Once the skills are mastered, the pyramid can be rearranged, but kept in the
same proportions, so that problems remain only the tiniest tip.

Children from the age of 3 (or older) can take part in Family Meetings.
Even a family of two can use the Family Meeting format.

START BY PRACTICING 'APPRECIATIONS'

- **Tip:** A true Appreciation is specific.
  Example: "I appreciate Mom being nice to me." (This is not specific and
  could be said to many others.)
  "I appreciate the chocolate chip and peanut butter cookies Mom made for
  my soccer team." (This is specific and could not be said to others at
  random.)
- **Tip:** Avoid criticism. Rely on modeling and practice to improve this skill.

NEXT, PLAN A FUN ACTIVITY

- **Tip:** Start with something as simple as planning an upcoming dinner
  menu, deciding upon a board or card game to play together, or where to
  go for a walk.

FINALLY, INTRODUCE THE AGENDA AND PROBLEM-SOLVING

- **Tip:** Remember: Family Meetings are **not** courtrooms.
  Focus on **Solutions**.

Enjoy Family Meetings and the
fast-fleeting years of your time together!

SKILL BUILDING FOR THE FAMILY MEETING

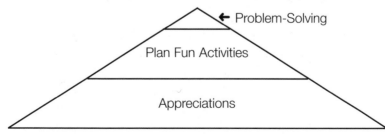

← Problem-Solving

Plan Fun Activities

Appreciations

Putting It All Together

Situation: Notes from the Field:
Positive Discipline Tools in Use

In the midst of teaching a six-week parenting class, I had the opportunity for some first-hand practice. Morning hassles are always hot class topics, so when my granddaughter spent the night and I needed to get her up and ready for preschool the next day, I decided to take some field notes.

Since I often write about using different tools as parents or caregivers, this was an opportunity to dissect which tools worked, when, how, or if they worked, and why I chose one over another. But first I need to preface my experience. Please remember that my morning had several special features.

*The first one was that this was **only one morning**. Let's face it, day-to-day is a different ball game.*

Secondly, I now operate under that unique 'grandparent mentality' that makes it possible to rationalize requests for milkshakes at breakfast with the thought that milkshakes do contain milk (not that I've actually served any breakfast milkshakes — yet!)

Thirdly, thanks to the blessings of hindsight I tend to forget the lost or missing shoes, coats, and car keys; my shrilly delivered reminders such as, "This is my last warning — Get Up NOW!" (those really didn't work!!); or the tears and recriminations from one child to another over who would get the last serving of the worst sugary cereal we ever made the repeated mistake of buying that frazzled our mornings during my children's growing up years.

These factors do give my field test morning a definite advantage over my previous day-to-day mornings with our four children. Nonetheless, the tools listed really can work and at least some of the time, especially when I remembered to use them, our real life day-to-day mornings often did flow rather well.

So sit back and join me on my morning field test, and be reassured that such mornings are possible in your lives, too. Be sure to congratulate yourselves on the one out of three days they happen and try not to pull your hair out or loathe yourselves (or your children) on the two they don't.

Task	What Happened	Tool Used	Comments
Wake-up	I snuggled next to her and whispered to her while she woke up.	**Special Time**	This set a soft tone for the morning.
Potty Time	She said she didn't have to go potty (Ha!). I said nothing and hugged her as we walked to the bathroom.	**Action** **No Words** **Kind and Firm**	Using the potty is a given for the morning, not something we needed to discuss (or argue about).
	She shook her head saying, "I don't have to." I said nothing.	**Ignoring**	I stepped back from a potential power struggle by not discussing the potty.
	I held up a tube of lip balm and asked if she wanted some. "Un-huh." "I'll put it on you while you are sitting on the potty."	**Distraction**	The lip balm effectively helped her forget she was resisting using the potty and once she was on it, nature took over.
	She sat on the potty and I turned the water on (it is hard to resist peeing when we hear running water).	**Alter the Environment**	The running water improved the likelihood that she would pee.
	I put on her lip balm. She peed. I beamed. More hugs.	**Encouragement**	The hugs kept us moving along and connected.

Task	What Happened	Tool Used	Comments
Getting Dressed	I held her on my lap and we chatted while I helped her out of her pajamas and into her clothes. I would do part of each task and she would finish it:	**Prevention (clothes already picked out)**	This is a real sticking point for most families. We want children to show independence and dress themselves, but what we often get are power struggles.
	I pulled her pajama bottoms to mid-hip and she wiggled them the rest of the way off.	**Special Time**	True, this was not a daily event for my granddaughter and me so holding her and helping her dress was a special treat.
	I put the shirt over her head and she put her arms through the sleeves, tugging her hair out of the collar.		The point is that it need not be all one way or the other and there is nothing wrong with making this a nice time to connect. Because the clothes were already laid out, there was no hassle over what to wear, which might have gotten us off track.
Eating	I asked if she would like waffles or sausages. She said, "No."	**Limited Choice**	This did not work. Time to switch tools.
	I set out a variety of foods in small portions. Then I got my own plate of food and told her breakfast was ready.	**Giving Choices**	By laying out a variety of foods I gave her the 'power' to select what to eat or not to eat. I left the decision up to her.
	She came to the table and ate small amounts of cereal, milk, apple, a granola bar, and sausage.	**Special Time** **Positive Attention**	No one likes eating alone, so sitting down with her gave us another chance to spend time together and for me to give her appropriate attention.

Task	What Happened	Tool Used	Comments
Getting Up with Food	When our cat came inside, she got up with her granola bar still in her hand and set off to chase the cat. I led her back to the table, pointing to the granola bar and her place at the table. She put the bar down and went off after the cat.	**Non-negotiable Rule** **Action** **Few or No Words** **Kind and Firm**	One rule in our house is that food must stay in the kitchen. She knows that rule so I didn't need to repeat it, only point to remind her. Even though she knows the rule, her limited *impulse control* and of course the appeal of the cat, made following the rule less important to her. I led her back rather than start a yelling match or lecturing, trying to get her to return. I decided what I would do, instead of what I would try to make her do. If she hadn't done so, I would have removed the granola bar from her hand (or she could have sat back down to eat it).
Potty before Leaving	She said she had to use the potty and went in and did so on her own.	**Nothing**	**Big Payoff:** all the tools put together equal = Self-Initiative

Task	What Happened	Tool Used	Comments
Tooth-brush Time	She asked to brush her teeth. I helped by providing the needed supplies. When she finished she smiled and said, "*I cleaned me.*"	**Prepared Environment**	**More Payoffs:** *Cooperation* *Self-Confidence* If this were a daily routine for us, we could have alternated turns with me doing some of the brushing. Because I want her to experience that feeling of '*I can do it!*' I wouldn't always insist on taking a turn or doing it for her. (*I believe self-esteem rates equal in value with the prevention of tooth decay. I hope no dentists are reading this.*)
Shoes and Coat	I got her foot into each shoe and she finished putting it on. I handed her raincoat to her. She took it and said, "Thank You," then put it on.	**Prevention**	I had the shoes and coat by the door, ready to go. **Payoff:** *Cooperation* *Show of Manners*
Good-bye	We hugged and kissed and I handed over her lunchbox. She walked out the door ahead of Grandpa, smiling and waving to me.	**Love**	**Payoff:** *A Great Start to the Day!* I will miss her. I hope she has a great day. She already made mine!
Tomorrow (or tonight or this afternoon) make each other's day — and have your own *Great Day*, too!			

THE 'TOOLS' DEFINED

Action: If you say it — do it — so be careful of what you say!

Cooperation: Many hands lifting a weight make everyone's portion lighter.

Distraction: 'Action' combined with something **new**, shifting attention in a different direction.

Firm and Kind: Think of a tree supporting a fragile bird's nest: the leaves give shade and protection from the wind and sun — that is **kind**. The trunk holds steady — that is **firm**. Trees do not get angry; that is the challenging part.

Limited Choices: Different options, all of which are acceptable. "Would you like to hug Grandma or do the Hokey-Pokey?" These would be effective limited choices, either of which I would love.

Love: The reason we are on the planet with others; also the blessing of children.

No Words: Silence.

Positive Attention: "I notice you. I am glad you are here."

Prepared (or altered) Environment: If you keep tripping on the same rug, in the same place over and over again, either toss the rug, tack it down, or dye it bright orange. If your daughter refuses to eat anything but marshmallows, quit buying marshmallows. It is the same principle.

Prevention: Be a fortune teller. Predict what might go wrong in a given situation. Prevent problems before they happen. If a child is too sleepy to wake up in the morning, get him to bed earlier the night before (I know this is easier said than done, but the principle is still true!).

Special Time: This is one-on-one time between people who care about one another. Time talks.

Tiny Drops: Kind and Firm Isn't Always Fun and Frolic

Situation: Kind and Firm Isn't Always Fun and Frolic

Not long ago, I wrote a column about getting our granddaughter, Mandy*, off to school after an overnight stay with us (see 'Putting It All Together' on page 333). One by one, I itemized the Positive Discipline tools and how each worked. Bonnie (a/k/a my editor) worried that I would discourage everyone with my picture perfect morning, so I added a caveat that although the tools work, things would not always be this smooth: my version of a 'Results May Vary' warning.

Well, this time, Grandma (me) and Grandpa (a 25-year veteran preschool teacher), the grand Pooh-Bahs of parenting, are about to make a lot of you feel really great! A large dollop of reality has humbled us.

Solution: Reality Check

The occasion was the birth of our newest granddaughter, Myra*, an event not regarded as blessed by one particular family member, i.e., her older sister, Mandy. Where to begin: before or after the eye drops?

Note: *To protect my grandchildren's privacy, these are not their real names.

I'll begin before. Mandy came home with her grandfather the night of Myra's birth, to spend the weekend at our house. This time the sailing was not so smooth. I will spare you the getting dressed, eating, and tooth brushing details, but suffice it to say that by mid-Saturday morning, we were well into our parenting tool bags. Where had our darling Mandy gone? It was like a different child had moved in and, of course, one had!

OPERATION EYE DROPS

Things deteriorated when, the morning after Myra's birth, Mandy was diagnosed with pink eye, thus triggering 'operation eye drops'.

Eye drops fall into that category of non-negotiable tasks, few of which are welcomed by either children or parents (or in this case, grandparents). The discipline challenge any of us face in these non-negotiable moments is that of acting in ways that are both 'firm and kind'.

FIRM AND KIND

My favorite image for this combination of **firm and kind** is that of a tree cradling a bird's nest. The tree is strong and reliable, both aspects of **firm** while it is also gentle enough to hold a fragile nest of eggs in its arms, a vision of **kindness**.

In real life, **firm and kind** can turn into what one parent calls **firm and mean**, with the splash of a cup of grape juice, while **firm**, especially in public, can be anything but fun.

Let's apply this in day-to-day terms around the dinner table. Imagine telling your child that if she plays with her food, you will assume she is through eating and ask her to clear her plate, or do so for her.

When, a few nights later, she begins juggling her peas (as I assure you she will) and refuses to clear her plate upon request (another almost certainty), performing the removal of that plateful of peas, mashed potatoes, and chicken wings will involve your hands lifting the plate and your mouth opening to say little beyond, "I see you have finished eating."

Both your actions and words would, of course, be **firm**; but keeping your feet from stomping or your mouth from scolding would be much harder. It is when we add the stomping or scolding that **kind** vanishes and **mean** appears.

There are also times when **kind** may not seem friendly. Seeing that a child gets enough sleep may prove a **kindness** to her and everyone around her the next day, but getting her to bed the night before in order to achieve that next day's **kindness** may not be much fun.

Doing something such as administering a medical treatment (in our case, the eye drops) may not seem very **kind** to the child on the receiving end, but allowing an illness to go untreated would be **unkind** to that child, as well as to any others exposed to her contagion.

WHAT WAS I THINKING?

All of which brings us back to 'Operation Eye-drops'. Being the confident and skilled parent (now grandparent) that I am, and knowing the importance of this **kind and firm** approach, I was fully prepared to be both. While the pharmacist filled our eye drop prescription, I guided Mandy over to choose a bouquet of flowers for her mother. All seemed well, even if Mandy could not be described as enthusiastic.

Next, wrapped in my own little bubble of optimism, I announced that we would apply the eye drops *right there at the store*. My husband struggled to hide his horror at this, while I took several deep breaths and gathered paper towels, "To wipe up any excess."

Then, steering our trio to the two brown plastic-covered chairs at the back of the store, with admirable **firmness** and positively oozing **kindness**, I said, "As soon as we get these eye drops in, we will all be able to go to the hospital to see Mommy, Daddy, and baby Myra." (HA! Fat chance!)

It took several minutes to convince me that not only were we **not** getting eye drops into Mandy's eyes, but that we were unlikely to get anywhere **near** those eyes and would have a good chance of being suspected of child abuse if we kept trying.

Firm plus **public** *did not equal* **fun***.*

With me clenching a wilting bouquet of flowers in one hand and Mandy's fist in the other, we returned to the car.

On the way back home, not to the hospital, I told Mandy that we would still need to put the eye drops in when we got to our house (non-negotiable, remember?). Aside from Mandy's sobs, it was a silent ride home. At that point, **kind and firm** felt just plain miserable.

HOME AGAIN
Once back at our house, we all needed to recuperate. We ate peanut butter and jam sandwiches, drank orange juice, and shared an apple. Mandy and I hugged, cuddled, and felt mutually terrible. Her eyes stayed pink and goopy. She still needed eye drops.

I tried reasoning. "It would be easier for all of us if you would cooperate," I said. Nice idea, Granny, but NO WAY!

In the end, it took the combined efforts of both 'Parenting Pooh-bahs' (a/k/a Grandma and Grandpa) to get those eye drops in, but we did; and thanks to much deep-breathing, we also managed to stay **kind**.

FROM MANDY'S PERSPECTIVE
The next day, and two more uncooperative eye drop applications later, we were relieved to hand over 'Operation Eye drops' to Mandy's parents.

On our way home, after re-uniting Mandy with her newly-expanded family, my husband summarized it this way: from Mandy's perspective, first we'd kidnapped her (taking her to our house the night of Myra's birth); then we'd held her hostage (while Mommy, Daddy, and Myra basked in the comforts of the 'hotel', Mandy's name for the hospital); then we'd tortured her (i.e., 'Operation Eye drops').

Hmm.

DOING OUR BEST

Could this have been easier on us all? Maybe. We have since unearthed a new eye drop application strategy: have the child close her eyes (that was no problem for us); squeeze the drops or cream onto the corner of each eyelid (near the nose); then watch the medicine flow inside when she opens her eyes (which she has to do eventually!).

Though this technique might have helped, I suspect we couldn't have accomplished anything with cooperation that weekend. There are times when that is the way parenting is: full of tasks no one likes, but that have to be done, anyway.

There are also times that all the experience, techniques, and understanding in the world don't work. We were firm (and kind), but it sure wasn't fun!

Sometimes that is the best any of us can do.

EPILOGUE

P. S. Two months later, Mandy and I are once again swinging in the hammock; singing with hearts (if not voices) in harmony; and dear baby Myra is doing just fine!

CONCLUSION

Different Paths

One day, after visiting my daughter at her new apartment (she is now grown, and along with her sisters and brother, have left their childhood and our shared home behind), we decided to go to a favorite Thai restaurant for lunch. We each took our own cars, setting out at the same time, but at the first large intersection — she turned left and I went right. We chose different paths and took our own preferred side streets, and yet less than ten minutes later, we rolled into the parking lot of the restaurant, side-by-side.

That trip with its common destination and different paths, seemed to be a perfect metaphor for the paths we travel as parents. Each of us, parent and child, is unique, which means that the twists and turns of our paths will also be unique. At times my children may have existed on peanut butter sandwiches (when they didn't like the night's dinner offering), and yet all of my children eventually became excellent cooks willing to try all kinds of foods. My friend counted popcorn as a vegetable, serving it on occasion with dinner, and yet her son went on to train as a successful, professional baker. Different paths — similar outcomes.

We all choose different paths, make different decisions, and have different beliefs driving our choices, but in the end, we try to do our best, or the best we each know how to do, as we travel through the various intersections life presents to us.

YOU DECIDE

It is my hope that this book has given you many possibilities — ideas to use as well as different ways to think about and look at the many situations that all parents of young children face. In the end, though we share many problems in common, we must each find the answers that best fit our hearts, situations, and families. The ideas in this book do work and will give you necessary tools to help you become the kind of parent you most want to be. Our shared goal is the same: we want to find connection, compassion, and respect for and with all of those whom we most love. It is a mutual destination.

FOREVER, NEVER, ALWAYS

I remember thinking that it was little consolation to be told that my first-born's colic would 'only' last six weeks because there was nothing 'only' about those six weeks — I was sure they would last FOREVER!

I carried a diaper bag around for so many years that I became positive I would NEVER leave home without it.

When our family would gather for each evening meal and one or another of them would grumble over what became known as my 'experiments' (I did and do have a weakness for trying new recipes), I would laugh along with them, knowing full well that we would ALWAYS be together, arguing over my chipotle flavored pastas, sweet potato enchiladas, or pizza-style potato entrees.

But FOREVER ended one day years ago when both my little one and I slept through the night for the first time as her colic melted away into 'only' a memory.

The diapers, too, were eventually gone and I NEVER gave a further thought to that unlamented diaper bag.

And, of course, those 'ALWAYS together' meals, too soon, have become the rare and precious times when we are all in the same place, instead of separated by miles or continents, as our children have grown up and moved on and away.

Throughout these pages we have explored the TOP TEN PRESCHOOL PARENTING PROBLEMS (AND MORE), but these early years truly do not last FOREVER and one thing I can promise you with certainty is that all of your problems, even when they seem NEVER-ENDING — will at some point, end.

These times together, like the problems they produce, won't ALWAYS be there — and will one day become 'only' our memories of them.

Do share your love for one another and fill these days with the very best kind of memories, for our memories of these times *will last FOREVER* and the love we have for one another will endure — for it is truly *NEVER-ENDING*.

Most importantly, we can *ALWAYS* be there for one another — even when 'there' spans miles, oceans, or continents. Whatever path you choose — may it take you and your family to safety, joy, and shared love; may your problems be even more fleeting than these fast-moving early years of childhood; and may your memories of these years fill your souls with a joy that is truly *NEVER-ENDING*.

Our children may grow into adults,
but we are their parents *FOREVER!*

INDEX

QUICK LIST OF TIPS, HINTS, CHARTS

ABOUT THE AUTHOR

ROSLYN ANN DUFFY founded and co-directed the Learning Tree Montessori Childcare. She is a lecturer, trainer, and workshop leader working with Early Childhood Educators and families around the world. A parent of four children and grandma to three, Roslyn lives in Seattle, Washington, where she heads the Better Living Institute and maintains a private counseling practice.

You may contact Roslyn at www.RoslynDuffy.com or by phone (206) 527-9728.